# THE PRIDE OF BEING

# A FAILURE

*(Unveiling the Mysteries of Failure and Success)*

## Joseph O. Ikwebe

**The Pride Of Being A Failure**

Copyright © 2021 Joseph O. Ikwebe

ISBN:

All rights reserved under international copyright law. No part of this publication may be reproduced or transmitted in any form or by any means electronic or mechanical, including photocopying, recording, or any information storage and retrieval system, without permission in writing from the author and publisher.

# DEDICATION

This book is dedicated to the Almighty God for His wisdom to write and to my pretty damsel Eunice Ene Adaora, my Lovely Wife Chioma Deborah Ikwebe and my late sweet Sister Rosemary Agwube Odang, and Late Sister-In-law Gift Ujunwa Alihie (Nurse Uju) for their love and supports. Also to those individuals who over the years have shared with me their personal struggles with failure and in so doing forced me to search for answers to the troublesome experience of failure.

# TABLE OF CONTENT

ACKNOWLEDGEMENT

INTRODUCTION

CHAPTER 1: Understanding Failure

CHAPTER 2: Understanding Success

CHAPTER 3: Why People Fail or Succeed

CHAPTER 4: Misconceptions & Myths about Failure

CHAPTER 5: Misconceptions & Myths about Success

CHAPTER 6: Habits that Enhances Failure or Success and How to Break Them

CHAPTER 7: How to Create Success Habits

CHAPTER 8: Personality Traits & Characteristics that Guarantees Failure or Success

CHAPTER 9: Regrets of Failure or Success

CONCLUSION

EPILOGUE

# ACKNOWLEDGEMENT

Few people want to admit that they have problem with failure. Most of us readily see the failure on the part of others, but seldom see it in ourselves. I want to acknowledge my debts to many people who in privacy of my interaction with them have shared their tendency towards their experience of failure. They realized that their negative methods of responding to failure were having a very destructive effect on their businesses and other endeavors of their lives, and they sincerely wanted help. Many came with the deep sense of guilt of being called failures.

Their openness therefore, forced me to give attention to the whole matter of understanding and studying failure in such a way that it can actually lead us to true success. Their willingness to be vulnerable has made this book possible. Without them, I would not have begun the search that led me to the discovery that failure actually has a very good and positive dimension.

I am also deeply indebted to Noah John, Ebenezer Jonah, Moses Alsun (Mr. 8), Ifeanyi Enegide, Pst. Success Akpan, Rev. Moses Okiki Adesina, Stephen Adzufeh and John Ovat who not only encouraged me in keeping on through the times of trials but also continued to pray and work with me to see that we all overcome failure and achieve success. You guys are the best of team members that anyone can ever dream to have.

Also to Pastor Bartholomew Oche, Amb. Michael Okoli and the entire Giant Team of the Century 21 Freedom Group International (C21FG), Mentor Habib Sunday, Mentor Olajide Alomaja, Mr. Nnamdi Obiechina and his Project 3000 Club International team, the Free Millionaires' Platform Members for their usual excellent job of encouraging, supporting, and guiding my efforts.

Mrs. Comfort Okpere assisted me greatly with her experience in publishing books online and Dr. Ahmed Isah (The Ordinary President of the Extraordinary Global Village) was my constant encourager.

Finally, I express my appreciation to my wife, Chioma, who has stood with me through the pain and joys of life. On this project, as with others, she could not have been more supportive. Never complaining about my late night hours on the computer. She always supported my efforts and prayed on my behalf. And my pretty daughter Eunice, who will always pray for me to make plenty of money anytime I leave the house for the office. I love you all!

# INTRODUCTION

*"I can accept failure,
everyone fails at something.
But I can't accept not
trying."*
**Michael Jordan**

The amount of time or years you spend here on heart has nothing really to do with your level of importance, but the amount or quality of impact you make during your time on earth.
A lot has happened in the world within the last few years. Among others, there was a global financial crisis; the impact was strongly felt in Nigeria and not too long ago the world fell into a global economic recession through the emergence of the Corona Virus also known as Covid-19.

In these years, unemployment has jumped to uncontrollable levels due to the inventions and the introduction of some robots. That has led to the government not being able to employ all our young graduates and all other unemployed people. It is therefore imperative for those who are unemployed and underemployed to find ways to engage themselves in one economic activity or another so as to add their value to the growth of the economy.

It is said that value is a product of impact. Therefore, Failure or Success are literally the sum total of your value on earth. So, to be valueless, equals failure and to be valueable or valueful equals success.

When you are successful it means you are impactful and you are a failure people regard you to be impactless.

I was moved to write this book to provide a simple guide for everybody who is willing and ready to succeed and create a niche for themselves. Therefore, what we need to create value and be able to absorb the large number of the unemployed in our society, is our desire to create new businesses, new entrepreneurs and new innovative ideas that can be put to work to help revolutionize our economy.

If half of the our unemployed people decides to create values by starting a business each, even if they are going to employ only themselves, that would mean a huge drop in unemployment in our society. This would in turn have a massive economic and socio-political impact on our society. But the fear of failure has being stirring them on their face and that is hindering them from starting.

This book has been written to encourage all those who can dare to create value. To be sure, not everybody can create value but nearly everybody needs where to be employed.

Without any iota of doubt, I believe that by reading this book, you will be tempted to launch out of the failure zone and determine to become a success.

I hereby wish you an unrecoverable experience, as you journey through the pages of this book to discover **THE PRIDE OF BEING A FAILURE**.

*JOSEPH O. IKWEBE*

# CHAPTER 1

# UNDERSTANDING FAILURE

*"It is impossible to live without failing at something, unless you live so cautiously that you might as well not have lived at all, in which case you have failed by default."*
J. K. Rowling

**DEFINING FAILURE?**

According to Merriam Webster Dictionary, Failure is a lack of success in some effort. It also defined Failure as a situation or occurrence in which something does not work as it should. It continued in by saying that Failure an occurrence in which someone does not do something that should be done.

While looking at it from Wikipedia, Failure is the state or condition of not meeting a desirable or intended objective, and may be viewed as the opposite of success. From this definition it also made to understand that the criteria for failure depends on context, and may be relative to a particular observer or belief system.

Having gotten the definition of success above, I will like you to know that *the greatest failure in life is being successful in the wrong assignment.* And trying to continue in the struggle to keep succeeding in that wrong assignment will lead you to a very destructive and regrettable end in time and eternity.

I therefore want you to know that your religion, background, tribe, qualification, occupation etc., has nothing to do with your state of being a failure or a success.

Most people tend to believe that poverty is failure and riches is success but the reality of the matter is that poverty is not failure and riches is not success. But poverty can only enhances the state or the character of being a failure; as well as riches being an enhancing tool for success.

So, I make bold to say that your level of success can be greatly determine by your level of riches and you can also become a failure when you are surrounded by poverty.

## WHY IS FAILURE SO IMPORTANT

The importance of failure cannot be over emphasized, but the fact still remains that until you come to the realization of failure as a basic building tool for your success, you've not began the journey to achieve any form of success.

Failure, no matter how it hurts, has a greater importance to life's journey than it's negative impact. I have failed more often than I'd like admit. And I'm not talking about small failure; I'm talking about the kind of failures that rocks your world, completely altering the landscape or your relationships, finance, and mental wellbeing. And, if you're anything like me, then it means that you've also most likely failed many times over. I can't say that I particularly enjoy failing, but failure through its life-altering lessons, makes us into better persons.

That is why I always make bold to say that ***"It's through failure that we learn the greatest lessons that life could teach us."***

## WHAT IS REALLY FAILURE?

What is failure really? Why is it so important to fail at something before we can succeed? This was the reason I began to dig deep into the research world and to ask the universe so much questions relating to what it means to fail and what it means to succeed. The outcome of those researches and questions brought about this timeless book you are holding and reading at this moment of your life. It took me a lot to realize that failure in the real sense is not the opposite of success but rather failure is the real sponsor and enhancer of success.

As a student of life, and a great learner of the universe, I have come to understand that my success in any outcome must be preceded by my failure in that same endeavour irrespective of how it happens to me. Until failure is able to reshape your thought system, your mind can never be properly reprogrammed for success.

When thinking about failure, we actually think of things in a negative light. We say that failure is painful and that it causes emotional havoc and upset, and inflict excruciating pains of guilt, regret, and remorse. But, for those that have known true failure, and have bounced back from it, they understand that failure in life is necessary for success. Sure, failing hurts. In fact, it can even cut deep like a razor, slicing its way to our inner core. Yet, it's necessary if we really want to experience success.

I have also learnt that the most successful people in life have failed the most times. If you try to go through life without failing at anything, then you're not really living a life at all. Taking risks and falling down flat on our faces is part of life; it creates us into who we are. The problem we are having in our society, is that people tends to celebrate the successes rather than highlighting the ambitious journeys towards success that are always filled with trials, tribulations, upsets, setbacks, and failures. It's not as glamorous to talk about those things that people go through to arrive at success because they seem not to be very interesting.

Still talking about failure, I want you to listen to this statement by one of the greatest basketballer that played that game and became a success: quoting him, he said *"I've missed more than 9000 shots in my career. I've lost almost 300 games. 26 times, I've been trusted to take the game winning shot and missed. I've failed over and over and over again in my life. And that is why I succeed."* - His name is Michael Jordan.

In life, it's therefore obligatory to fail. Failure is a bridge. In fact, there are five (5) very powerful life lessons that failure helps to teach and instill in us. If you've recently failed at something in a major way like me, and you're going through a difficult time right now, keep these important lessons in mind.

1. **Experience**

   According to Wikipedia, Experience is the process through which conscious organisms perceive the world around them. It states that experiences can be accompanied by active awareness on the part of the person having the experience, although they need not be.

   Looking at it from the Merriam Webster Dictionary, Experience is a practical knowledge, skill, or practice derived from direct observation of or participation in events or in a particular activity. It also went ahead to explain that Experience is also the length of time that you have spent doing something such as a particular job.

   The above definitions has clearly taking care of the fact that the way you perceive the world around you can be accompanied by active awareness on the part of the person having the experience. It also made us understand that the quality of our knowledge, skill or practice derived from direct observation of or participation in a particular event and the length of time we spend doing something has also to do with our level of success or failure in life.

2. **Knowledge**

Looking at it from Wikipedia, Knowledge is a familiarity, awareness, or understanding of someone or something, such as facts, skills, or objects. It states that by most accounts, knowledge can be acquired in many different ways and from many sources, including but not limited to perception, reason, memory, testimony, scientific inquiry, education, and practice.

According to Merriam Webster Dictionary, Knowledge is the fact or condition of knowing something with familiarity gained through experience or association. It also explained Knowledge as information, understanding, or skill that you get from experience or education.

Failure has always brought with it a very important firsthand knowledge. This knowledge which is the experience and skill gained can then be harnessed in the future to turnaround that very failure that inflicted so much pain in the first place. I have not seen anything in this world that can replace the knowledge gained from failure. For instance, when Thomas Edison famously failed nearly 10,000 times to create a commercially viable electric lightbulb, it was said that with each failure, he gained the knowledge of just one more avenue that the electric bulb didn't work. It was the accumulated knowledge developed from nearly 10,000 failed attempts that ultimately led to his success.

3. **Resilience**

According to Merriam Webster Dictionary, Resilience is the capability of a strained body to recover it size and shape after deformation caused especially by compressive stress. It also defined Resilience as the ability to become strong, healthy, or successful again after something bad happen.

In physics, resilience is the ability of an elastic material such as rubber or animal tissue to absorb energy such as from a blow and release that energy as it springs back to its original shape.

Failing in life therefore aids to build our resilience. The more we fail, the more resilient we become. Our ability to recover from defeat has a great deal of helping us to arrive at success. Because, if we ever think that we're going to succeed on the first try, or even the first few attempts, then we're sure to set ourselves up for a far more painful failure. Becoming strong, healthy, or successful after something bad happens can eventually help us in so many ways in life. Always remember that every success in life will take a very serious effort to achieve it.

4. **Growth**

Growth according to the Merriam Webster Dictionary is a stage or condition in increasing, developing, or maturing. It also defines it as a natural process of increasing in size or development.

Growth is a proof that we are developing and becoming matured in whatever we found ourselves to do. It is pertinent to know that when we fail, we grow and mature as human beings. It is therefore when we fail, that we reach deeper meanings and develops better understandings about our lives and why we're doing the things that we're doing. It helps us to reflect and take things into its proper perspective, thereby developing meaning by us from painful situations. Life itself was designed for us to grow and improve in every aspect of our career. It is therefore vital to know that without growth we cannot be able to improve life on every front.

5. **Value**

According to Merriam Webster Dictionary, Value can be defined as worth, usefulness, or importance in comparison with something else.

Looking at it from Wikipedia, Value denotes the degree of importance of something or action, with the aim of determining what actions are best to do or what way is best to live, or to describe the significance of different actions.

Earlier on in this book, we were made to understand that value comes as a result of the impact that we generate or contribute to our society. So, one of the predominant lessons that we can learn from life's failures is the necessity and ability to create and spread an exceedingly high amount of value. The lack of value in itself is the fundamental pillar that leads to failure. So, when thinking about your past failures, first of all settle down and think about how much value you brought to the table. Ask yourself these questions, what experience, knowledge, resilience and growth have you brought into it; ask yourself if I could have applied all the experience gathered, put all the knowledge I had to work and recovered from setback by becoming more matured, would that have prevented failure? Always have it at the back of your mind that whenever you learn to create immense value, and do it consistently, your outcome will eventually lead you to success.

**Ways to Recover From Failure**

There are a quite number of ways to recover from failure. But the understanding of what failure is, and how it's meant to serve us rather than obstruct us, will eventually free our mind and open our heart to experience the joy that is contained in failure.

Do I say Joy? Yes! I said Joy. Because whenever we're going through failure, it's actually very hard to recognize the importance of it. The avoidance to recognize the forest through the trees has nothing to do with us, but when fire begins to threaten to burn down the whole village, we begin to value and know the danger of the trees around us. That's just what we have to do. So, if you've ever experience any form of failure in life, you should better understand that there is an importance in failing and not just failing but failing often.

Now let us look at some ways to recover from failure? Although there are so many ways to recover from failure but I will mentions a few ways in this book:

1. **Ignore the Pessimists**

    Whenever we fail or attempt something new, there are always a certain group of people that will be telling us, ***"It won't work,"*** and things like ***"You should have listened to me."*** Always ignore those people. I repeat, always ignore the pessimists. Because what they are always trying to do for you is to establish you in the realm of wanting or loving to exist in the safe mode, which in reality is not good for you if you must become a person of great success. If you have ever watched J. K. Rowling's Harvard commencement speech (which I strongly recommend you to look for it and watch it), then you will surely understand what it means to walk away with a better understanding of how to ignore the pessimists.

2. **Have the Understanding that it's not a Bad Thing to Fail**

One of the best ways to recover from failure is to understand that it's quite alright to fail. If you are to conduct a search on the web today on the benefits of failure, you would find countless stories about failure from the world's most successful people who have failed in life at one time or another. That makes me to be bold to say, It's okay to fail. But on the contrary, it's not okay to give up. Even if you failed and that failure was extremely painful, it's not okay to give up. Just keep failing over and over again if you have to. The refusal to give up is the key to keep on doing it until you succeed. I want you to know that success will taste so much sweeter when you reach it.

So, pushing forward and not giving up is possibly one of the best ways to recover from failure. Remember, it's not true failure unless you decide to throw in that proverbial towel and wholeheartedly decide to give up forever.

3. **Realize that the Pain of Failure cannot be compared to the Gain of Success**

Even though failure to us symbolizes pain, and we'll always do more to avoid pain than we will do to experience the gain of success, we have to come to the point of realizing that the pain of failure cannot be compared to the gain of success. Like I mentioned earlier, realizing the importance that failure had played in the lives of the most successful people in our society, positions you for a better understanding of it. I want you to know that failure will take you on a journey that you might not want to go on. But, the reality of the situation is that those journeys will help to mold and shape you into a better person in your society.

Therefore, recovering from failure becomes far more effortless with the knowledge and experience that we get by having the failure controlled under our belts. It is now clear that there's simply no other way in enjoying the gains of success in life without the pains of failure.

4. **Learn to use Failure as Leverage**

Leverage in this context means gathering enough skills and knowledge as debts from your previous failure, which will enable you to overcome any new challenge that will come to you in the future. If you've ever failed in life before, you can then use that as leverage to not only recover from failure, but it will also help to propel you forward in the future towards achieving success. Failure itself can be a great platform for growth that is simply unmatched. To leverage your failures therefore, you have to write out what you failed at and why you failed. You've to know if you had deep enough meaning to your goals in the past. What could you have done differently? How will you tackle those failures in the future when you're faced with them again? How will you learn from the past to help shape a bigger and brighter future for you?

I want you to know that failure isn't the end of the road as long as you don't give up. The only thing that will make you to leverage properly from your past failure is to believe in your goals. When this is done, you can then use the failure as leverage to push past the old limitations of your past failures.

5. **Revisit Your Goals and Visions**

How solid was your goals and visions in the past? Did you set goals the SMART way? Was your goal **S**pecific, **M**easurable, **A**chievable, **R**ealistic and **T**ime bound? Just try to revisit you goals from the past and look at just how clear you were with your goals. Were they precise and exact? Did you visualize them in your mind? Most times, failure results from not setting goals the right way. Not only must we set goals the right way, but we must track and analyze them on a monthly, weekly, and daily basis with the proper understanding of the SWOT of our visions. How was the **S**trength of your vision? Was there any attention given to the **W**eakness of the vision? When the **O**pportunities came knocking, were your there to harness them? Did you ever think of the **T**hreat that will come your way during the periods of the said vision?

If your answers to the above mentioned questions are no, the better way for you to recover from failure therefore, is to revisit your goals and redefine them. You will need to spend enough time to analyze and adjust your goals and vision where necessary, so as to recover from failure.

6. **Creating or Developing a Massive Action Plan**

Recovering from failure cannot be done with perplexity or laxity. You must be willing to Create or Develop a Massive Action Plan that will enable you to properly track your goals and visions. It requires taking your goals and laying out a definite action plan as to how you're going to achieve them. Determine what you will do in the face of failure next time when it rears its ugly head? Whenever we create or develop a massive action plan, it enables us to have a systematic way of achieving the goals that we set for ourselves. Once we come to the realization that those goals and visions won't be simple to achieve, we can then approach things with a more durable way of overcoming failure or achieving success.

Always endeavour to set out a solid and massive action plan that will help you push past the stumbling blocks of life, and watch as you slowly but surely recover from any setbacks, upsets, or failure.

# CHAPTER 2

## UNDERSTANDING SUCCESS

*"One of the fundamental key to success in any field of endeavor is learning to establish priorities and then living by them."*
**Joe O. Ikwebe**

### DEFINING SUCCESS

Success is a very vast subject of discussion that we cannot just take a few pages of this book to explain but to enable us attain some form of greatness or impact, we will discuss the little we can do in the cause of this book. Let us now begin by first understanding the definition of success.

### WHAT IS SUCCESS?

According to Wikipedia, Success is the state or condition of meeting a defined range of expectations. It may be viewed as the opposite of failure. According to this definition, one person might consider a success what another person considers a failure, particularly in cases of direct competition or a zero-sum game.

The definition of success cannot be over emphasized but looking at it from the Merriam Webster Dictionary, Success is the fact of getting or achieving wealth, respect, or fame. It went ahead to let us know that success is someone or something that is successful.

Here are some perspectives you need to know in order for you to re-evaluate the importance of your journey from failure to success:-

### 1. Success requires some level of the Impact of Suffering

Now, one thing that everyone must go through at some point in life, is **Suffering**. According to Wikipedia, Suffering or pain in a broad sense, may be an experience of unpleasantness and aversion associated with the perception of harm or threat of harm in an individual. It continued to explain that Suffering is the basic element that makes up the negative valence of affective phenomena. By this, it concludes that the opposite of suffering is pleasure or happiness.

Although, this is a harsh reality, yet we cannot actually avoid it in its entirety. We most times experience suffering as the result of unhappiness, fear, anger, loss or frustration. In fact, it would be hard to even imagine the feeling of happiness if we never experienced any suffering! But how would we ever compare it? Now instead of wallowing in sorrow about the suffering you have endured for a very long time, decide to take the suffering as an opportunity for your desired change.

## 2. Success requires the Impact of Self-Talk

According to Dictionary.com, Self-talk is defined as the act or practice of talking to oneself, either aloud or silently and mentally.

Self-talk can either be positive or negative. Many times self-talk may arise from some misconceptions that people create for themselves or from an experience gotten from a given suffering. Others could come from external sources such as negative people around you, or messages from the media. But the key factor that will make the impact of self-talk work for you correctly is to surround yourself with positive influences that can help turn those negative thoughts into positive and more productive actions.

You'll not only begin to feel better about the situation, but in the long run, positive thinking can lower your levels of distress and depression and position you to get a better handling skills during hardships and trials.

## 3. Success Requires Your Attitude

According to Wikipedia, Attitude is a psychological construct, a mental and emotional entity that inheres in, or characterizes a person. It also continues that those attitudes are complex and are an acquired state through experiences.

Looking at it from the Merriam Webster Dictionary, Attitude is a bodily state of readiness to respond in a characteristic way to a stimulus (such as an object, concept, or situation). It also define attitude as the way you think and feel about someone or something. And that it is also a feeling or way of thinking that affects a person's behaviour.

With the above insertion, it is therefore clear that attitude is everything when it comes to achieving a goal, and tackling a setback or problem. So, whenever you're able to have a positive mindset, you'll be able to break free of your restrictions that are holding you back. Attitude is therefore the key to your lasting and total transformation.

**4. Success requires the Impact of Gratitude**

According to Merriam Webster Dictionary, Gratitude is the state of being grateful. It also defined it as a feeling of appreciation or thanks. But looking at it from the Cambridge Dictionary, Gratitude can be defined as a strong feeling of appreciation to someone or something for what the person has done to help you.

Gratitude is a very useful tool when you're trying to navigate your way out of a setback. Having gotten that precise understanding from the above-mentioned definitions, it is pertinent for me now to say that being grateful, even during the toughest of times, steers up your attitude towards a more positive one, thereby allowing you to get back on your feet much more quickly. There are studies that have shown that a higher motivation in a work setting has a lot of improvement in relationships and mental health if it is practiced regularly.

**5. Success requires You to Believe in Yourself**

According to the Merriam Webster Dictionary, Believe is to have a firm conviction as to the goodness, efficacy, or ability of something. It also continued that Believe is to have faith or confidence in the existence or worth of something.

Looking at it from the Dictionary.Com, Believe is to have confidence in the truth, the existence, or the reliability of something; although without absolute proof that one is right in doing so.

When it comes to believing yourself, it is easier said than done, but it's really the most empowering truth to devastating your setbacks and limitations in life. Just setting your goals in life and being positive that you will achieve them. I know people who doubt their abilities because of the **'failure'** that they're experiencing, and don't even think that they can rise above it again. Confidence comes from overcoming difficulties and facing your fears head on. Confidence is therefore a result of getting out of your comfort zone.

Here's a quick story about my own struggles helping me get ahead:

When I first started Jorex Integrated and Global Resources Int'l, organizing free personal development and success trainings, it took a long time to gain a solid followership. Just getting 50 people was a challenge and it took a good bit of time. I had great ambitions for this platform, yet it seemed like I was doomed to fail. I received plenty of criticism too. Some people thought that the world didn't need yet another self-help platform, others offered the opinion that there was something wrong with the idea itself and I was making a mistake. It was hard for me not to listen to them and, at sometimes agree. But, persistence and consistence are vital keys and in the end I chose to believe in my truth. I worked tirelessly changing the platform formats, restructuring methods, and making the platform more users friendly. Slowly, I expanded to a team with the inclusion of some extremely dynamic and talented people. With each determined effort, the platform grew in popularity, and a few years later, we have so far influenced some people, we've created other platforms that we now use to train and develop people and will continue to do so.

Pushing myself out my comfort zone and facing every challenge head on were the greatest contributing factors to increasing my confidence. So welcome to the world of challenges because they will surely come; but my advice to you is, never try to avoid them, as they're all opportunities in disguise to feed your growth.

In conclusion of this chapter, I want you to know that you are your greatest barrier to success, which is why it's very important to always believe in yourself! If you do this, you will always have the power to be in control of your situation because your attitude is determined by you!

# CHAPTER 3

# WHY PEOPLE FAIL OR SUCCEED

*"The greatest enemy of knowledge is not ignorance; it is the illusion of knowledge. So your refusal to learn something new today, will establish you in a state of slavery to someone who did when tomorrow appears."*
**Joe O. Ikwebe**

According to Wikipedia, Failure is the state or condition of not meeting a desirable or intended objective, and may be viewed as the opposite of success. But looking at it from the Merriam Webster Dictionary, Failure is a situation or occurrence in which something does not work as it should. It also defined it as an occurrence in which someone does not do something that should be done.

However, if you're finding yourself failing a little more often than you would like, it might be time to address some issues such as those that were mentioned earlier in the previous chapters and those that would still be mentioned later as we journey through this timeless book.

Here are some top ten reasons or mistakes why people fail, and how to possibly fix them to attain success:

1. **You need to look before you leap**

    The matter of looking before leaping is a very crucial aspect that must be considered if we are going to talk about the reason why people fail or succeed in life, career, family or business. For example, starting a business without looking at the business first. This will eventually set you up for failure, instead of you just waking up to start a business or any career line, I advice you to learn from a professional and practice until you feel ready to perform before launching into the marketplace.

2. **You need to know the level at which you need it**

    Grow or success in any endeavour is determined by the level or the depth of its foundation. The foundation for success is therefore laid from the experiences we learn or gather from our various failure endeavors. Knowing the level at which you need it; will set the pace for how it will definitely happen in the real life. Your level of want is what attracts the amount of result that will come your way in real life. So, if you want something, you are going to really want it bad enough for it to come to you in reality. This will in turn motivate you to do your absolute best.

3. **You need to know when to look for alternatives**

According to the Merriam Webster Dictionary, Alternative is a proposition or situation offering a choice between two or more things only one of which may be chosen. It is also an opportunity for deciding between two or more courses or propositions.

So knowing when things are not working out and deciding to tackle it from a different angle is what determines either your failure or success. Because you might just be surprised how many things you could accomplish if you just tried approaching it in a slightly different way than it normally looks. This will in turn give you a completely new perspective and might even end up in success.

4. **You need to know when to give up**

According to the Merriam Webster Dictionary, to give up means to cease doing or attempting something especially as an admission of defeat.

Are you in the categories of people, whom failing once means never trying again? Then I want you to know that there's a lot to be said for those who will definitely bounce back and keep trying. It shows persistence which is the quality that allows someone to continue doing something or trying to do something even though it is difficult or opposed by other people. And in oftentimes lead to success. So, don't get too discouraged after failing once or twice, just keep going and you're more likely to get what you want by existing beyond the usual, expected, or normal time.

5. **You need to have a SMART Goal**

According to Wikipedia, A Goal is an idea of the future or desired result that a person or a group of people envision, plan and commit to achieve. It also explained that a Goal is roughly similar to a purpose or aim, the anticipated result which guides reaction, or an end, which is an object, either a physical object or an abstract object, that has intrinsic value.

You cannot succeed in any endeavour if you don't clearly know what you want from that particular field or endeavour. If you haven't defined what constitutes a success to you, you won't be able to reach it. Make sure you have a very clear idea of what success means to you. In terms of Goals, your success therefore must be **S**pecific, **M**easureable, **A**ttainable, **R**ealistic, and **T**ime bound that is where we got the acronym SMART from. By setting your success priority along with this five desired outcomes, you have a concrete goal in mind and by following or working towards it, you will eventually reach the peak of your career in life or business.

6. **You must heed to advice from successfully proven professionals**

   Learning and listening to those who have been in your shoes in the past can be very helpful. Always reach out to those who understand what you're going through and have accomplished what you're working towards. Because they are the ones that can tell you the pitfalls to avoid at every given stages of your journey to success. The piece of advice they will give you might just change your entire view of the problem and position you for a better productivity in your society.

7. **You must avoid listening to too much advice from failures**

   As I often tell people around me, *"that it is stupidity for you to sit down listening to a poor man trying to teach you how to become rich."* Same it is when the matter of failure and success is concerned. There's no teacher in this world that would ever teach you beyond his level or capacity of knowledge. So, listening to too much advice at once from failures can get you confusing. Don't ever limit yourself to a handful of people who actually don't know what they're talking about. There are chances that, many people who are trying to dole out advice don't even know much about the subject. So my advice to you as a reader of this timeless book is to only seek help from people who know exactly what you're going through and have the skill set to talk about that topic confidently.

8. **You must learnt to avoid giving too many excuses**

According to Merriam Webster, Excuse a reason that you give to explain a mistake, bad behaviour, etc. It also define Excuse as reasons that you give to explain politely why you cannot do something, why you have to leave, etc.

Excuses can only get you a little far. Instead of making excuses as to why you're failing, try thinking about what the real reasons are for your failure and begin to work on them positively. Because, the sooner you face these reasons, the sooner you can get back on track to success. Always address any major issues and make sure you get back on your feet as rapidly as possible.

9. **You must avoid the attitude of talking but no show**

It is said that too much analysis leads to paralysis. There are some people who will always talk a big game but will never follow through with any genuine action. Please, don't be found in those categories of people. Yes, you should always endeavour to plan and talk things out with others, but don't let that get in the way of you not actually taking action. The Holy Books in Proverbs 10: 19 (NLT) says ***"Too much talk leads to sin. Be sensible and keep your mouth shut."***

10. **You must learn not to misjudge**

According to the Merriam Webster Dictionary, to misjudge means to have an unfair opinion about someone or something. It also explained Misjudge as a way to estimate something, such as an amount, distance, etc. incorrectly.

I want you to know that Times and Seasons are changing rapidly. So, it will be an error for you reading this timeless book right now, to be cut in the web of the office of the Chief Misjudge of the universe. Also know that in times of difficulty and monetary investment, such as the one we are in at the moment, a lot of people fail because they have refuse to do their homework properly. Before you engage in any project in this season, make sure you know what you're getting into and always overestimate to give yourself some ease and level of freedom from embarrassment.

## IS THERE ANY PRICE REQUIRED FOR STARTING ALL OVER AGAIN?

The answer to the above question is No! But the lack of this understanding is the reason why so many people are afraid of attempting any big venture that will eventually see them experience any form of failure. Where you failed last is where you will be meant to start again even if you wait for another one hundred years to come before you start.

There is no single law on the universe that has set any given price for you when you start all over again. Starting is starting whether it is a fresh start or it is to start all over again. The only word the universe hears and responds to is the word **START**. In other words all you need is to take the action that is required and the universe will be there to assist you.

Let's take an instance from the Motorcar engine, when you come out of a car for some hours and you decide to go back into that same car to start it, will you be required to pay or do anything special before starting the car engine? The answer is a very big and capital NO! As it is with the Motorcar engine, so it is with the universe that we live. You are only limited to the capacity or level that you are willing to be limited.

I challenge you to dare try something new today and see how the universe will respond to you quickly and as fast as possible. Every great inventions and discoveries that we enjoy today in our world was first a mere product of idea but when it was ready to be transformed as a material outcome, the universe supported them and gave them every necessary support that they needed to make it a reality.

Anywhere you are in the world right now, and you are reading this timeless book, I challenge you to dare something bigger than your level of knowledge, and see whether the universe will not support you provided all the needed ingredients are on ground and accessible by you to successfully carry out or execute your so called big project.

See you at the top friends!

# CHAPTER 4

# THE MISCONCEPTIONS AND MYTHS ABOUT FAILURE

*"Failure will never overtake me if my determination to succeed is strong enough"*
**Og Mandino**

## MISCONCEPTIONS ABOUT FAILURE

According to the Merriam Webster Dictionary, Misconception is defined as a wrong or inaccurate idea or conception. In another way, a misconception is also a conclusion that's wrong because it's based on faulty thinking or facts that are wrong.

My own understanding of the word Misconception is, whatever you accept into your mindset, decide to store it in your subconscious mind, and then work around making people to believe that it is true when in reality it's nothing but a big LIE.

These are internal self-defeating garbage. It can be either positive or negative depending on how you take it.

Here are some misconceptions about failure that are very popular and are often used by people around us:

1. **Failure is Bad:**

    Let's say you attempt to implement a new marketing system and it fails to produce effective results. You probably learned something in the process, but the facts remains that the project failed. So failure is not bad or good but rather an outcome of an unplanned action or decision. Refusing to move on after experiencing failure is makes you a failure. But if you get up, dust yourself off and continue to fail, you'll continue to learn and eventually implement something that work and stand the sands of time. By this logic, failing is a good thing. It is just for you to learn to fail small, fail early, and fail often, because the lessons you'll learn along the way will be invaluable.

2. **Failure is the End, I am completely defeated:**

    Nothing in this life other than death is an end. Failure should rather be our teacher, not our undertaker. Failure is a delay, not a defeat. It is a temporary alternative route, not a dead end. Failure is something we can avoid only by saying nothing, doing nothing, and being nothing. Failure is never the end. The Holy Book says: *"For surely there is an end; and thine expectation shall not be cut off."* (Prov. 23:19 KJV) When you choose to believe in God, you will soon discover that failure is not the end but just a new beginning. So try again and never quit at the first attempt.

3. **I have failed; maybe I am not good Enough:**

This is clearly another big lie. Failure doesn't mean you are not good enough. You are much more good and you were wonderfully created. So you can still achieve great things. In fact, you are created unto good works and not unto failure. If you don't try your ability at anything, you can't really fail... All you need to do is just change your mindset that you are good enough for it, then go for it. And success will be your new name.

4. **I am afraid I will fail again if I try:**

I want to make you understand today that fear and failure always go hand in hand? Don't be afraid. Fear is often interpreted as **F**alse **E**vidence **A**ppearing **R**eal. According to Jack Canfield, *"Everything you want is on the other side of fear."* Taking a critical look at that statement, you will realize that it is not failure that is actually limiting you but fear. So, if you dare to try again, you will see that you will not fail again. Success only belongs to those who try and try and try again and again. Let's consider these quotes by **Thomas Alva Edison** who has been described as America's greatest inventor. He developed many devices that greatly influenced life around the world, including the phonograph, motion picture camera, and the long-lasting practical electric light bulb. He says, ***"Genius is one percent inspiration and ninety-nine percent perspiration." "I have not failed, I've just found 10,000 ways that it won't work."*** He also said, that ***"Many of life's failures are people who did not realize how close they were to success when they gave up."***

5. **Failure is Fatal:**

This is another misconception, but I want you to always believe that your failure is not the worst thing that could even happen to you. That is when you will begin to see things starting to turn around for your success. According to John Worde, ***"Failure isn't fatal, but failure to change might be."*** So, decide to change today and your story will also change for good.

6. **God does not Love me that's why I failed:**

One of the biggest misconceptions about failure in my own opinion, is when you feel you failed because God does not love you. That is the highest form of deception that could ever exist in this world. In fact, discouragement and defeat are key negative emotions that you should always watch out for. The only way these negative emotions can be turned to positive emotion for you, will be based on your decision to know and have a proper understanding of God's love for you. (See John 3:16; 1 John 4: 7–9) The fact that you failed does not in any way mean that God has abandoned you.

7. **Failure is the end of the World:**

Failure cannot be, and is not the end of the world. Because if you can just decide to change your mindset from believing on that false assumption, It can become a new beginning for you. Failure shows one what does not work. It is said that Edison had thousands of failures with the incandescent light bulb. However, he refused to give up on what did not work, until he happened upon the one thing that did work. Failures are merely the ways you learn to readjust what you are doing or striving for.

In conclusion on the matter of misconception, I want you to embrace each failure as a temporary state of being, an opportunity for significant self-improvement and never a permanent destination. Experience failure and always milk it for all it's worth, but never concede to it.

## SOME COMMON MYTHS THAT SURROUNDS FAILURE

Having being able to get rid of some internal self-defeating garbage and misconceptions that has kept us in a perpetual mental imprisonment, let us now go into it in a more practical way. By now, I know we've decided that we are going to refuse being identified or recognized as failures. That's the first step and a very important one at that. This makes us to exist in a realm of freedom that automatically helps us to take the next step and start working towards our dreams, goals, and visions.

## WHAT IS A MYTH?

According to the Merriam Webster Dictionary, A Myth is usually a traditional story of ostensibly historical events that serves to unfold part of the world view of a people or explain a practice, belief, or natural phenomenon. It is also a popular belief or tradition that has grown up around something or someone. Let me add this, that Myth is a person or thing having only an imaginary or unverifiable existence.

In refusing to be identified as a failure, we've therefore saved ourselves from activating fear. In order to understand failure, we therefore need to look at some common myths surrounding failure.

### #1: **Failure is an Identity:**

According to Wikipedia, Identity is the qualities, beliefs, personality, looks and/or expressions that make a person or group. One can regard the awareness and the categorizing of identity as positive or as destructive. A psychological identity relates to self-image, self-esteem, and individuality.

Looking at it from the Merriam Webster Dictionary, Identity is the distinguishing character or personality of an individual. It also defined Identity as sameness in all that constitutes the objective reality of a thing.

I want you to know that our identity does not really lie in who we are. But it actually lies in **Whose** we are. Therefore, having the understanding that your soul was purchased with a pretty hefty price; the sacrifice of God Himself incarnate on the cross. That's where our identity comes from. Having this understanding makes me to be certain that God would not single-mindedly pursue someone whom He considered to be a failure. But He would rather, however, pursue someone that people consider to be a failure. That was one the reason why Jesus spent a whole lot more time with society's *"failures"* than he did with society's so called *"successful"* people.

The world and the men in it can label you as a failure, but what authority do they really have to make that judgment? Until you accept that as your identity, you can never become a failure.

We've all been given complete and ultimate hope in our lives. So, if I can really trust in God for my salvation, then I should also trust Him with my identity as well. He's good enough to cover both. Therefore, I always choose to risk failure each and every day. I will continue in reckless pursuit of God's will for my life. Because that is the only way I can fulfill His Divine Mandate upon my life.

Even if I will start a few new businesses along the way. I know some of them will fail. But I will continue to forge ahead and make new relationships as I go. I know several of those relationships will fail as well; I'll do some crazy stuff that will make you all think that I am certifiably insane. I might even make a few mistakes that will cost me everything. That's all just fine, because that's the only way I'm going to become exactly who God wants me to be. But no matter what, I want you to refuse to be identified as a failure. Just know that being afraid to fail is really the foundation of remaining a failure in life.

#2: **Failure is the same thing as failing**

Let's say you attempt to implement a new empowerment or investment system just like what I did in the cause of my journey from failure to success and it fails to produce effective results. You probably learned something in the process, but the fact remains that the project failed. If you failed once and refuse to move on, then you have truly experienced failure.

On the contrary if you get up, dust yourself off, and continue to fail, you'll continue to learn and eventually implement something that works. By this logic therefore, failing is a good thing. So, if you learn to fail small, fail early, and fail often, the lessons you'll learn along the way will be invaluable. And that will make you to clearly know that there is a very big difference between failure as a thing and failing in a thing.

### #3: **Failure is Subjective**

You must decide to make Failure to be objective and not subjective. The myth that failure is something that you need to be subjected to is a very wrong belief. Always endeavor to define your facts and figures so as to identify your absolute breaking point. Because if you don't define what failure looks like in your life, career, family or business, your ego will definitely do it for you. Your fragile ego will always let your life spring all the way down the drain before it admits defeat. At this point, you'll find yourself cashing in all your investments, selling your valuables, and taking out loans to finance an already packed up business. This is happens when your failure becomes a lot. And this only happens when you refuse to differentiate between failure as an object and failure as a subject.

### #4: **Failure is Deserved**

Please I want you to always endeavor to check any self-defeating attitudes at the door. Because, you do not deserve to fail! Neither does your life, family or business deserve to fail. If you start out on this journey with the idea that you don't deserve to succeed, I promise you that you won't. So, always do your due diligence research, and craft your business plan, then give it 150% action. Don't ever try to phone it in. But always work your tail off to create some remarkable things. Your model or method may be considered imperfect. The market may reject your idea. Things might just not work out for you. Don't ever think for a second that your social status, personality, worldview, or anything else of that nature caused you to deserve failure. Always remember that God's plan for you is to prosper you in all realms. (see Jeremiah 29:11 AMP)

## #5: **Failure is a Step Backwards**

Backward is said to be the opposite of forward. But I want to let you know that Failure is neither a step backward or forward. Because you can either fail forward or fail backward. Failure can happen in both directions as long as you are alive and still breathing. The understanding you have about failure and success will determine the direction that either of them will take you. If you understand either of them to be a step forward, that it will be for you and if you understand it to be a step backwards that it will also be for you. So, the belief that failure is a step backwards is nothing but a mere statement of fact, the truth is not contained in it.

## #6: **Failure is Evil**

For me, I will say that Failure is neutral. It is just a response to an action that we take or a decision that we make. To me, Failure even seems to be very benevolent. Because failure only responds to the actions that we take or decisions that we make in response to a given outcome. All you need to do is to go back to the drawing board with a new understanding and a new mindset. So as to really create that new plan that will really work for you.

### #7: **Failure is Fatal**

This is one of the most important myths that we need to throw light on when talking about failure. We need have a significant paradigm shift here, because ***"failure is not Death. But Failure is rather Birth."*** So, Failure is not fatal. Failure is just a temporary state of being where we think that we have lost everything but in the reality, we have actually not lost anything. Failure only gives us the very opportunity that we need to get back to the basic and work on the stuff that actually matters to us rather than begin to accept defeat and begin to decline in life.

So to move forward therefore in life, we need to embrace each failure as a temporary state of being; we need to see it as an opportunity for significant self-improvement and never a permanent destination.

# CHAPTER 5

# MISCONCEPTIONS AND MYTHS ABOUT SUCCESS

*"The trouble with the world is not that people know little;
it's that they know so many things that just aren't so".*
**Mark Twain**

According to Wikipedia, Success is the state or condition of meeting a defined range of expectations. It may be viewed as the opposite of failure.

Looking at it from the Merriam Webster Dictionary, Success is the fact of getting or achieving wealth, respect, or fame.

Believing that success requires some specific conditions or is meant for a certain category of people is a very big LIE. So learning to always avoid such misconceptions will help you to grab the success that can be yours!

Now, let us enumerate few of these misconceptions of success that has kept so many people in a perpetual slavery:

1. **Some people can't be successful because of their background, education, etc**

    Success has nothing to do with either your background, education, religion, sex or even marital status. Success is a universal outcome to the obedience of a given law. To know what is right and do it in the proper perspective is what I normally refer to as success.
    Success does not require any special skill, background, or education to experience it. All it requires is your willingness and readiness to follow a certain laid down principles that will lead you to achieving and enjoying its benefits.

2. **The most Successful people don't make mistakes**

    To hear people say that successful people don't make mistakes always baffles me because as a student of failure and success, I have realized that mistakes are vital requirements or building block for attaining any level of success in any life's endeavour. Successful people take a lot of action, make a lot of mistakes, and then make corrections. It is your ability to learn from your mistakes that makes you become successful. Every successful person make mistakes just like we all do. The only difference is that they just don't repeat them.

3. **Success requires a lot of hours each week**

    Actually, it is very possible for you to be incredibly successful and still maintain a reasonable schedule. The key factor here, is to spend your time on the most important tasks.

Most people spend or waste too much time on activities that really don't matter. So, it's not a matter of doing a lot of something. But it's rather more about doing the right thing that will yield fruit or results.

4. **You'll only be a success if you play by the rules**

Success is a matter of achieving simple actions and determining what works and then working hard enough to repeat it. If we say that that success can only happen if we play by the rule, then who actually makes these rules? Every situation in life requires a different approach. Although sometimes following the rules is needed, but other times making your own rules is what matters. I want you to always have it in mind that success is more about persistence than the brilliance knowledge of a given rule.

5. **If you have help along the way, it's not success**

Trying to be successful alone, is dramatically accepting to slow down your own progress. Every single human being on earth was designed to be helped or render assistance to another person at a given point of time. So therefore, accepting that you don't need help to achieve success to me is remaining at the lowest form of failure. Every successful story I have ever heard about in this world has something to do with the building of a very good team that worked together to achieve that success. So you need people's help, if you must be successful in life.

6. **It takes a lot of luck to be successful**

In as much as how it sounds to be true, that it takes a lot of luck to be successful. Success on its own has nothing to do with luck but rather hard work. So, all you need is to put the amount of work that is required to produce success, and will definitely become successful.

7. **It's only successful if you make a lot of money.**

Money is just one of many benefits to success, but it's not the only guaranteed. There are many people who have a lot of money yet are not successful. So use your head!

8. **Once I'm successful, my troubles are over.**

To be successful does not in any way exempt you from the troubles of this life. Because even if you are very successful, you should also remember that you're still a human being and not God. So, you'll still experience the ups and downs that you did before. For that reason, just enjoy what success you have achieved and live each day as it comes.

9. **Success is determined at birth**

This is one of the misconceptions that have kept so many people in the state of frustration for a very long time as a result of what they think should be success to them that turned out to become failure. That you are born to a certain family does not guarantee that you will become automatically successful in every endeavour that you engage in because many of the most successful people had the fewest advantages in the beginning of their lives.

10. **Successful people end up alone**

Except what you call success is not truly success, else the social opportunities for successful people are really mind-blowing. So in the real sense of things, it is unsuccessful people that end up being alone. (See Proverbs 14:20 MSG)

11. **You can slack off once you've reached the top**

If you ask any successful person you know what it takes to remain at the top, he will tell you in all sincerity that the same principles that you obeyed to leave the bottom level is also require even with more severity at this point to help you remain at the top. So, you don't reach success and begin to slack because once you allow the results to overwhelm you, be ready to loose your success with reckless abandon. You need to avoid being complacent to stay and remain on top.

So many of the beliefs regarding success that you know may be actually false. But you need to believe and know that it is not only few people that are capable of becoming successful. The truth is that success is always available to anyone with the focus and determination to be successful. So always endeavour to avoid these common misconceptions and decide to make a decision to succeed.

# CHAPTER 6

## HABITS THAT ENHANCES FAILURE OR SUCCESS.
## HOW TO BREAK THEM

*"Remember your dreams and fight for them.*
*You must know what you want from life.*
*There is just one thing that makes your dream*
*become impossible: the fear of failure."*
Paulo Coelho

### WHAT IS HABIT

According to the Merriam Webster Dictionary, Habit is defined as a behaviour pattern acquired by frequent repetition or physiologic exposure that shows itself in regularity or increased facility of performance. While Wikipedia defines Habit as a routine of behavior that is repeated regularly and tends to occur subconsciously. The American Journal of Psychology defines a habit from the standpoint of psychology, as a more or less fixed way of thinking, willing, or feeling acquired through previous repetition of a mental experience.

With the above definitions, it is very clear to us that habits are not just things that we do that we know but things that we don't even know that we are doing that people around see and judge is based by them.

With this in mind, it won't be out of place for us to try and identify some high performance habits that will help us to achieve our goals of becoming successful. So, let's consider the following habits to being successful as listed on the table below:

| Failure Habits | Success Habits |
| --- | --- |
| Unrighteousness | Righteousness |
| Foolishness | Wisdom |
| Doubt | Faith |
| Lack of Purpose | Purpose/Pursuit |
| Lies | Truth |
| Laziness | Hard work |
| Consumption | Investment |
| Isolation | Mentoring |
| Mediocrity | Excellence |

I will be giving the explanation and interpretation of the above-mentioned habits based on my understanding and how I applied them to attain success out of failure.

## THE FAILURE HABITS

We are going to start with left side of the table which are the Failure habits. Every habit that is enumerated here has in one way or the other imparted me in my quest of migrating from failure to success. These habits has nothing to do with either being positive or negative in nature. All I know is that the refusal to recognize and handle properly any of these habits will either make you a failure or help you to leave the realm of failure.

Let's begin our voyage:

**UNRIGHTEOUSNESS:**

This is a failure to adhere to moral principles. I won't have the time to go too deep in explaining what unrighteousness is but the fact remains that any success endeavour that you engage without the Source of Life (God) Himself is prone to automatic Failure. So, you need God if you must be successful in life. There's no two ways about it!

**FOOLISHNESS:**

According to Wikipedia, Foolishness is the unawareness or lack of social norms which causes offence, annoyance, trouble and/or injury. The things such as impulsivity and/or influences may affect a person's ability to make otherwise reasonable decisions. In this sense, it differs from stupidity, which is the lack of intelligence.

Let's see how the Cambridge Dictionary defines it. It defines Foolishness as the quality of being unwise, stupid, or not showing good judgment.

Even though the above definitions are self-explanatory, I would like to inform you that if there's any endeavour that you are currently struggling with, and not getting the kind of results that you desire, you should be aware that there is a level of foolishness that you are either displaying or refusing to recognize.

## DOUBT:

According to Wikipedia, Doubt is a mental state in which the mind remains suspended between two or more contradictory propositions, unable to be certain of any of them. It may involve uncertainty, distrust or lack of conviction on certain facts, actions, motives, or decisions. I don't know about you but for me, anything that I lack conviction about, I either cease doing it, or decide to learn from a proven professional or books about all that is necessary for me to know to gain the convictions in order to operate very well in that realm.

## LACK OF PURPOSE:

According to the Merriam Webster Dictionary, purpose is something set up as an object or end to be attained. And it defined lack as the fact or state of being wanting or deficient. So going by these definitions, we can now make bold to say that the lack of purpose is the fact or state of being wanting or deficient in something set up as an object or end to be attained. To lack purpose therefore is to be deficient of purpose. As Dr. Myles Munroe of Blessed memory said: *"when the purpose of a thing is not known, abuse is evitable."*

I don't think it will be wrong for me to say that lack of purpose happens when purpose itself is abused.

If you don't have anything that is driving you towards success, then it should be clear to you that you are already heading to the realm of failure and this comes as a result of refusal to take responsibilities as at when due.

**LIES**:

Wikipedia defines a Lie as an assertion that is believed to be false, typically used with the purpose of deceiving someone. The practice of communicating lies is called lying. And a person who communicates a lie may be termed a liar. To Lie also is to make an untrue statement with intent to deceive.

I want you to examine yourself at this point and ask yourself this simple question: Are mine deceiving myself to my own detriment? Or Am I lying to other people by trying to create a false or misleading impression about me? The answer you give yourself will prove to you whether you are a failure or not.

**LAZINESS:**

According to Wikipedia, Laziness also known as indolence is disinclination to activity or exertion despite having the ability to act or to exert oneself.

To be termed a lazy person is to be unwilling to work or be active; Laziness can also be described as a state of moving slowly. Laziness makes you to lose your enthusiasm and energy. As a result the person also happens to lose all opportunities and finally becomes dejected and frustrated. Most lazy people tend not to take chances, but express themselves by tearing down other's work.

## CONSUMPTION:

This is the act of consuming, as by use, decay, or destruction. It is also the action of using up resources. In our contemporary societies today, consumption rather than saving has become the central feature of the day. This has created a manic world sick with the pursuit of material wealth. For this reason, many people now bear their cross of imagined deprivation, while their fellow human beings remain paralyzed by real poverty. Though this is not always mentioned to our ears, but the fact still remains that existing only to be a consumer is to exist as a total failure in life.

## ISOLATION:

According to the Merriam Webster Dictionary, Isolation is the state of being in a place or situation that is separate from others. It is also the act of separating something from others. Based on my level of understanding, this state of being alone or lonely always leads to depression and frustration. I also want you to know that no one can live without relationships. It is either we allow our ignorance to prevail upon us and make us think we can survive alone, alone in patches, alone in groups, alone in races, even alone in genders. But the truth remains that you can make more friends in two months by becoming interested in other people than you can in two years by trying to get other people interested in you. Decide where you belong today!

## MEDIOCRITY:

According to the Merriam Webster Dictionary, Mediocrity is defined as the quality of something that is not very good: it is the quality or state of being a mediocre. A Mediocre is a person who does not have the special ability to do something well.

I want you to know that becoming a person of good quality, requires you to excuse yourself from the presence of shallow and naive minded individuals. I don't know about you, but based on my experience so far in the journey of success, I have realized that Mediocrity often makes you either disagreeable or intimidating by creative people. The resultant outcome of this is that, Jealousy becomes the tribute mediocre people pay to genius.

## HOW TO BREAK THESE BAD HABITS

According to the Merriam Webster Dictionary, To Break means to separate into parts with suddenness or violence. It also mean to invalidate a will by action under the provisions of the law. It can also mean to find an explanation or solution for something or someone. I also want you to know that to Break out of something is the action or act of entering, escaping, or emerging from something (such as darkness) often in a sudden or violent way. This can also be referred as the act of breaking in, breaking out, or breaking forth.

I took out some time above to enumerate and make us understand some meanings of what it means to break because, all the habits of failure that we mentioned earlier are mechanical tasks automated by our brains or simply said habits. And all habits fall under the same laws and rules of creation and destruction.

As I learned how to destroy and break habits and I applied that to the ones in my life. They didn't only work for me, I've shared the way with a couple of people including my friends and it worked for them too. So the process which I will describe in this book will work for you too, if only you decide to apply them.

It's now time to get rid of those troublesome bad habits that establishes you in failure:

1. **Working on Your Environment**

    According to the Merriam Webster Dictionary, An Environment can be defined as the conditions that surround someone or something. It is the conditions and influences that affect the growth, health, progress, etc., of someone or something. To further buttress it, Environment is the aggregate of social and cultural conditions that influence the life of an individual or community.

    Learning from experience, I have discovered that the very first step to breaking any form of habit either good or bad is changing our environment. It's as a result of this change in environment that you encounter a lot of toxic, negative and failure based reactions. But always have it in mind that the only thing that is permanent in life is change and that includes even environment.

So, any environment you found yourself, that the activities there is either limiting your efforts or diminishing your results, requires an urgent action for change. It could either be you that is not compatible to the environment or the activities of the environment that is not compatible with you. Either ways, movement is urgently required for a better outcome.

2. **Starting Small, As Small As Possible**

Starting anything new including the change of habits can be a herculean task, but starting it as small as possible is the key to experiencing a great level of change in that endeavour. To start small you need to first make up your mind that you want to start and nothing on earth should be so powerful enough to make you stop what you started.

I still remember vividly when I decided that I want to become a Personal Development Coach, it was such a very big task for me to change from the normal 9am to 5pm a day kind of job. There were so many reasons that required me to quit and continue my normal life. But whenever I think of the impact that my trainings and materials such as this book you are reading now will do in the lives of people, I decided to sacrifice everything to achieving that very important change in my life. Today, it's no longer a strange terrain for me but when I started initially, it was not easy going at all. So, I challenge you too today to make up your mind and start that journey for change in that area of your life that you still need success.

3. **Track and Measure you Outcomes**

According to YourDictionary.Com, To track means to monitor the progress of something, to follow behind something or to try to find something. It can also means a specific area on which something is to take place or that has been designed for a specific purpose. While to measure according to the Merriam Webster Dictionary, is to judge the importance, value, or extent of something.

What I did that help me overcome and sustain the change I started was first to monitor the progress I was making, then follow behind and try to find that thing which was designed for that purpose. After sometimes, I discovered that success has already set in, I then decided to choose, control, and restraint myself to a certain degree that I began to realize that the change I was looking for has already been established, then I forged ahead to start another small venture and so on and so forth.

4. **Changing Your Identity**

Let me start here by saying, that identity defines people and deeply informs and gives meaning to every aspect of their lives. So as your belief system is changing, your identity too should also change.

According to Wikipedia, Identity is the qualities, beliefs, personality, looks and/or expressions that make a person or group. It also explained that one can regard the awareness and the categorizing of identity as positive or as destructive.

Looking at it from the Merriam Webster Dictionary, Identity is the distinguishing character or personality of an individual.

There's therefore no reason why you should still allow your old failure and self-defeating habits to have an upper hand over your life. This can be made very easy if we really decide to track and measure our progress in every given areas of our lives.

Today I may be known with a new identity, but that was not a default identity. I decided to first work on my environment, then started as small as possible, tracking and measuring every moves or activities that I engage in. when all of these was in place, my identity had no option but to change automatically.

All these four ways were instrumental to the success of my migrating from the failure realm to the successful realm. So, without any iota of doubt, I sure know that it will help you break those bad habits of failure too.

## THE SUCCESS HABITS

Having enumerated some habits of failure, let us now take a look at some habits that can also help us to attain or achieve success. These habits includes the following:

**RIGHTEOUSNESS:**

According to Wikipedia, Righteousness is the quality or state of being morally correct and justifiable. It can be considered synonymous with rightness or being upright. To be righteous means to act accord with divine or moral law. In other words, to be righteous means to be free from guilt or sin.

With the above understanding, I will now make bold to say that one of the greatest attributes that sustains a successful habit is righteousness. I don't want to delve into any religious matter or details, but I want you to know that the most successful people we have on earth are righteous people. (See Proverbs 14:34)

**WISDOM:**

According to Wikipedia, Wisdom, sapience, or sagacity is the ability to think and act using knowledge, experience, understanding, common sense and insight. It continues to explain that Wisdom is associated with attributes such as unbiased judgment, compassion, experiential self-knowledge, self-transcendence and non-attachment, and virtues such as ethics and benevolence.

As you seek to create successful habits, I adjure you to seek for wisdom, because Wisdom is what qualifies you to handle, manage or co-ordinate information, riches or glory that is greater than your size or age. So, I make bold to say that it is therefore wisdom that qualifies you for grace in any area of endeavour. Wisdom brings discipline and discipline is the bridge between goals and accomplishment. No man was ever wise by chance. Any wisdom you have for any successful venture that is not from God is fake.

**FAITH:**

According to Wikipedia, Faith derived from Latin *fides* and Old French *Feid,* is confidence or trust in a person, thing, or concept. It further explained that Religious people often think of faith as confidence based on a perceived degree of warrant, while others who are more skeptical of religion tend to think of faith as simply belief without evidence.

As you strive for success habits, I want you to know that faith is one of the basic necessity that will enable you to stand and overcome trials. To buttress that further, I also want you to always remember that all things are possible for those who believe. So, believe in yourself! Have faith in your abilities! Without a humble but reasonable confidence which is faith in your own powers you cannot be successful or happy in any endeavour.

**PURPOSE/PURSUIT:**

According to Merriam Webster Dictionary, **Purpose** is the aim or goal of a person. It also defined it as what a person is trying to do, become, etc. It then went on to say that Purpose can also be the feeling of being determined to do or achieve something.

Every successful person I have ever come in contact with, live a purpose driven life. What do I mean, they are very cautious of the fact that every second counts and for them to properly utilize those seconds, they have their days, weeks, and years properly mapped out even before it arrives. So, doing likewise will not only make you successful, but it will make you to exert enough dominance on your habits.

**PURSUIT:**

Looking at it from Merriam Webster Dictionary, Pursuit is defined as the act of following or chasing somebody. According to Dictionary.Com, Pursuit is any occupation, pastime, or the like, in which a person is engaged regularly or customarily.

Being persistent in the pursuit of our deepest destiny will continue to make us to grow. Even though, we cannot choose the day or time when we will fully blossom. We should come to the understanding that it will happens in its own time. We will never get our fulfillment in the pursuit of happiness but in the happiness of pursuit. So therefore, not engaging in the pursuit of ideas is to exist like ants instead of living like men.

**TRUTH:**

According to Wikipedia, Truth is the property of being in accord with fact or reality. It also explained that in everyday language, truth is typically ascribed to things that aim to represent reality or otherwise correspond to it, such as beliefs, propositions, and declarative sentences.

Looking at it from the Merriam Webster Dictionary, Truth is a statement or idea that is true or accepted as true.

Every successful person that you see, understand that the only way to continue to benefit positively from the universe is to remain truthful. Being truthful therefore positions you to receive from the universe the right element that will enable to succeed in every endeavour that you embark on. The truth is, we all face hardships of some kind, and you never know the struggles a person is going through before arriving at success. I also want you to know that behind every smile, there's a story of a personal struggle that often brings us to an idea that is either true or accepted to be true. Truth is therefore like the sun, it rises in the morning and shine during the day radiating it's scotch of heat on mankind and then decides to set in the evening. So, you can try to shut it out for a time, but it ain't going away. This therefore means that truth in its reality is not for all men, but only for those who seek it!

**HARD WORK:**

According to YourDictionary.Com, The definition of hard work is something requiring lots of efforts to do, either physical, mentally or emotionally.

Every successful person knows that hard work is the basis for everything worthwhile that you will achieve in life. But, to me, hard work is the process of physically and mentally exerting efforts in other to change both the world and yourself so that at the end you and the world have to become more real to other observers. So following the definition we saw earlier, it the amount of efforts we exert physically, mentally and emotionally that determines our level of success in the world and there no other way to go about being successful than being hardworking.

## INVESTMENT:

According to the Cambridge Dictionary, Investment is the act of putting money, effort, time, etc. into something to make a profit or get an advantage, or the money, effort, time etc. used to do this.

In an economic sense, an investment is the purchase of goods that are not consumed today but are used in the future for the purpose of creating wealth. In finance according to Cambridge Dictionary, Investment is the act of putting money into a business to buy new stock, machines, etc., or a sum of money that is invested in a business in this way.

As you determine to create the habits of success, I adjure you to endeavour to learn and practice what you learn properly when it comes to investment. This is because what you eat today does not benefit you much but, whatever you keep or invest for tomorrow has the capacity to multiply and grow beyond its original form. Every wise and successful person that has ever existed or pass through this universe has a better understanding of investment and that is what has lead them to the inventions, innovations, discoveries, theories and laws that has shaped the universe that we are living in today. Always remember that investment is the act of giving time or effort to a particular task today in order to make it successful in the future.

## Different Types of Investment

When it comes to investment, we cannot exhaust its importance and value as it relates to our secrets and quest for achieving success. So, there are various types of investment, or asset classes that you can choose from each with distinct characteristics, risks and benefits. But in the course of this book, we shall be looking at six (6) basic types of investment. And once you are familiar with the different types of assets, you can now begin to think about piecing together a mix that would fit with your personal circumstances and risk tolerance towards attaining success.

1. **Growth Investing:**

   According to Wikipedia, Growth Investing is a style of investment strategy focused on capital appreciation. It states that those who follow this style, known as growth investors, invest in companies that exhibit signs of above-average growth, even if the share price appears expensive in terms of metrics such as price to earnings or price to book ratios.

   This is scenario where you can invest in small or young companies whose potential earnings are expected to increase at an above average rate compared to their industry sectors or the overall market with the sole aim of increasing the investor's capital. These are usually more suitable for long term investors that are willing and will be able to withstand the ups and downs of the market.

2. **Shares:**

According to Wikipedia, in financial markets, Share is a unit used as mutual funds, limited partnerships, and real estate investment trusts. It also explains that Share capital refers to all of the shares of an enterprise. It went ahead to continue that the owner of shares in the company is a shareholder of the corporation.

To own a share also qualifies you for receiving income from your dividends. Shares can also help to grow the value of your original investment over the medium to the long term basis. Shares are classified into two types being **common shares** and **preferred shares**. A share can be issued by a company as a means to raise money for the future development and bigger reinvestment into the company or for the benefits of the shareholders. Shares also known as equities, have historically been proven to deliver a higher returns than other assets, because of this, shares are usually considered to be one of the riskiest types of investment.

3. **Property:**

According to Merriam Webster Dictionary, Property is a quality or trait belonging and especially peculiar to an individual or thing. It also defined it as something to which a person or business has a legal title. It also continue to explain that Property is a piece of land with buildings on it that is owned by a person, business, etc.

In my journey through failure to success I have come to realize that property is any physical or intangible entity that is owned either by a person or jointly by groups of people or even a corporation. So depending on the nature of the property in question, an owner can decide to consume, sell, rent, mortgage, transfer, exchange or destroy it or to exclude others from doing it with a legal right. So anything that is tangible or intangible whereby a legal relationship between persons and the government enforces a possessory interest or legal title in is referred to as Property. This is the reason why every successful person chooses to buy real estate and wait instead of waiting to buy real estate. However, just like shares, property also has the potential of falling in value and it carries the risk of a very big loss. But this happens most time only in rare cases.

4. **Defensive Investment:**

According to investopedia.com as written by James Chen, A Defensive Investment is a conservative method of portfolio allocation and management aimed at minimizing the risk of losing principal. He went on to say that a Defensive Investment strategy entails regular portfolio rebalancing to maintain one's intended asset allocation; buying high-quality, short-maturity bonds and blue-chip stocks; diversifying across both sectors and countries; placing stop loss orders; and holding cash and cash equivalents in down markets. These strategies he said are meant to protect investors against significant losses from major markets downturns. Since these forms of investment are more focused on consistently generating income, rather than growth they are considered lower risk than growth investments.

5. **Cash:**

According to Wikipedia, in economics Cash is money in the physical from of currency, such as banknotes and coins. In bookkeeping and finance, Cash is current assets comprising currency or currency equivalents that can be accessed immediately or near-immediately. But looking at it from the Merriam Webster Dictionary, Cash is money or its equivalent (as check) paid for goods at the time of purchase or delivery.

At this point as it relates to investment, I want you to know that even though cash typically carries the lowest potential returns of all the investment types, and that they offer no chance of capital growth, they can easily deliver regular income and can play very important role in protecting wealth and reducing risk in an investment portfolio. So positioning yourself to access cash at every given time as the need arises is not a crime but do not carry beyond the amount that is required for you to carry by the laws of your country or state.

6. **Fixed Interest:**

According to Investopedia.Com as written by Carol M. Kopp and reviewed by Marguerita Cheng, A Fixed Interest rate is an unchanging rate charged on a liability, such as a loan or mortgage. She says it might apply during the entire term of the loan or for just part of the term, but it remains the same throughout a set period. Then looking at it from Wikipedia, A Fixed Interest rate loan where the interest rate doesn't fluctuate during the fixed rate period of the loan. It continues to state that this allows the borrower to accurately predict their future payments. And that variable rate loans, by contrast, are anchored to the prevailing discount rate.

To my understanding, the best known type of fixed interest investments are bonds, this is situation in which government or companies borrow money from investors and pay them a rate of interest in return. Bonds are also said to be considered as a defensive investment, because they generally offer lower potential returns and lower levels of risk than shares or property. They can also be sold relatively quickly, like cash, although it's of a great importance to let you know that they just come without the risk of capital losses.

## MENTORING:

According to Wikipedia, Mentorship in which a more experienced or more knowledgeable person helps to guide a less experienced or less knowledgeable person. It went on to state that the Mentor may be older or younger than the person being mentored, but they must have a certain area of expertise. This is a system of semi-structural guidance whereby one person shares their knowledge, skills and experience to assist others to progress in their own lives and careers. Mentors need to be readily accessible and prepared to offer help as the need arises, within greed bonds.

As a student of life, I have learnt that every single thing I want to do or project I want to embark on, there is someone that has already passed that same process and had succeeded. So the only thing that the universe requires of me is to go to that person and ask for proper direction and advice as to how I can also navigate through it without any stress. The process of agreeing to submit to the instructions and also allowing such a person to guide and lead you through the required process involved in helping you arrive at success is what I call Mentoring. Mentoring is not in any way counseling or therapy, but even though the mentor may help the mentee to access more specialized avenues of help if it becomes apparent that this would be the best way forward, the both parties must play their parts very well to be able to arrive at success at the end.

So as a Mentee, being able to change/achieve your goals more quickly and effectively than working alone, is by building a network of professionals to draw from their expertise in such a way that it can benefit both yourself and others.

And As a Mentor, I want you to know that Mentoring is voluntary but it's extremely rewarding, and can benefit your own skills development and career progression. So, you need to be the sort of person who wants others to succeed, and have or can develop the skills needed to support them to grow in the right direction also.

**What is the Impact of Mentoring?**

Even though mentoring can make a profound difference to the lives of mentees, and in turn strengthen our communities, economy and country. Because the consistent, enduring presence of a caring adult in a young person's life can be the difference between staying in business, deciding to throw in the towel, making healthy decisions or engaging in risky behaviors and between realizing one's potential or failing to achieve one's dreams.

I have also learnt that young people with mentors especially tend to have more positive visions of themselves and their futures than those who tend to do it for themselves. They also achieve more positive outcomes in school, the workplace and their communities.

Every good mentor will assist you in making realistic plans and objectives for improving your effectiveness and developing your potential, they also give you the opportunity to reflect and challenge your own thinking, encourage greater adaptability and willingness to change and providing constructive feedback on your goals. A good mentor will also allow the luxury of allowing you to talk to an independent unbiased confidante who is not your competitor; they also possess the ability to listen to your issues and afford you the opportunity to escape wrong decisions and also support you in achieving your goals.

So, every mentee must be aware that mentors, are not there to find you a job, to solve all your career problems, they are not meant to be your workhorse or there to be your new best friend. But, every experienced mentor will share with the mentee their lessons learned and any relevant insights that the mentee may benefit from when confronting life or career issues.

## EXCELLENCE:

According to Wikipedia, Excellence is a talent or quality which is usually good and so surpasses ordinary standards. It also states that Excellence is also used as a standard of performance as measured e.g. through economic indicators.

Looking at it from Dictionary.Com, **Excellence** is the state or quality of excelling or being exceptionally good; extreme merit; superiority. It also states that Excellence is an action, characteristic, feature, etc, in which a person excels.

When it comes to excellence, it is often said that ***"If you cannot do great things, do small things in a great way."***

One of the greatest attributes that is common every person of success excellence. Excellence enables you to be sophisticated and equipped for better performance at every given time. Even though achieving excellence is never easy to do but possessing it makes you to operate in good qualities and that in very high degree. Excellence is a quality that almost everybody really tends to appreciate, because it's so hard to find. Excellence is the quality of excelling; it makes you to truly become the best at everything that you do. So, whenever and wherever you see excellence at work, you should always endeavour to appreciate the work that went into it because so much in the world that we live in most times falls short of excellence.

# CHAPTER 7

# HOW TO CREATE SUCCESS HABITS

> *"And once you understand that habits can change, you have the freedom and the responsibility to remake them"*
> **Charles Duhigg**

When we talk about how to create success habits according to Merriam Webster Dictionary, To Create means to produce or bring about by a course of action or behaviour. It also states that to create means to make or bring into existence something new. And looking at it from the Dictionary.Com, to create, is to cause to come into being, as something unique that would not naturally evolve or that is not made by ordinary processes.

So, if you are sitting around waiting for success to happen to you, then you have to really make it come to you. Because we're talking about how to create some success habits in your life. This will in turn improve your productivity, creative thinking and more importantly, your work-life balance and mental health.

Since you've battled with your failure habits, and have known some ways on how to break them, it's now time to create some success oriented habits that will catapult you onto the road to success. But first, you must decide to define what success really means to you before you can go ahead to create the habits that are associated with it. Having said all of the above, let us know find out what success is to us before we can continue. Is success more money to you? Is it Learning and acquiring new skills as much as possible? Or is it a particular promotion in your current job? Is success a way of life for you? Once you've been able to figure out what your success in life are, you can now use the tips below to create good habits that will get you there.

1. **Put Pen to Paper**

    Having decided to truly succeed, you'll need to create some reachable, measurable goals. Because it's not enough to say: *'I want to be this and that by next year.'* Even though the universe will be willing to pave the road for you, but yet you have to decide what route you will take to arrive at your destination, and that will be marked out in measurable goals that you can achieve and keep track of.

    Therefore, writing down these goals, gives you the key to realistic achievements. Don't ever forget to keep yourself accountable for those goals and decide how you're going to get there. Aside from committing your goals to paper to solidify them, telling yourself that you will be able to achieve those goals and believing in your abilities will get you closer to them.

2. **Measure Success in Happiness Rather than Wealth**

Endeavour to make your success bring you happiness rather than just accumulating wealth. This will now represents a shift in the way that you measure your success, because I have realized that many people define their success in terms of the amount of Pounds, Euro, Dollars and even Naira that they have accumulated in their various bank accounts or investment port folios. This kind of mindset only leads you to consistently chase a higher amount without ever achieving true satisfaction. And this can be counter-productive, so, I advise you to be sure to create a clearly defined vision of success and understand precisely what it means to you.

3. **Challenge yourself and Do Hard Things**

One of the first things you need to do to create success habits, is to first enable to achieve some level of personal growth. This in turn demands a willingness to accept and overcome difficult challenges. It is only when we learn to how to handle and overcome the obstacles around us that we can now be able to learn and develop critical life skills as well as success habits. It is therefore these attributes that will equip us to obtain success. I want you to know that it is by challenging yourself and confronting difficult tasks that you can also change your mind-set with regards to the possibilities that life holds for both you and your success.

4. **Learn to Embrace Failure**

Now that you have learnt that failure is considered to be one of the greatest teacher of valuable life lessons, drawing from painful and disappointing experiences therefore is far easier said than done. But the fact remains that it requires an ability for you to be able interpret the exact lessons that you have learnt from every individual failure that appeared to you. This will enable you to apply these lessons learnt in your quest for future success. By confronting the issue head on and identifying exactly where things went wrong, you can now take actionable steps towards ensuring that the same mistakes are not repeated again.

I also want you to know that failure might seem to be like a strange habit to include on the road to success, but the truth here is that failure is inevitable when it comes to achieving success. Even though you're still going to make mistakes in life, you're still going to fail at some things; you might even fail at forming some of these good habits. However, you must make sure that you create a habit of embracing every failure, obstacle and mistake and turning it as a learning opportunity. Choosing therefore to embrace failure and see it as a positive thing is one of the most difficult good habits that you can form, but it is one of the most important habits that will assist you to become successful.

5. **Develop a Consistent Wake-Up Routine**

Even though recent studies have suggested that not enjoying eight hours of sleep each day may actually be counter-productive to your levels of mental agility, but it is still very important that you develop a consistent cycle of sleep. This will enable you to become an early riser who wakes up at exactly the same time each day. This makes it far easier for you to optimize your time and develop a very good and productive schedule. This makes you to be awake while the rest of the world is still snoozing in bed.

Always know that your mornings are very powerful! And that's the reason why some of the most successful people in the world have committed morning routines that they never skip. It doesn't have to be getting up at 5am to make a protein-filled drink and going for an hour-long jog. It just helps in deciding how to best wake your body up to get ready for the day's activity.

Whatever the routine is, be sure to committing to never missing it for no single reason. I will also advise you to always write down your goals for the day in the morning before leaving the house for the office. Whatever you therefore decide your routine to be, the fundamental key is to keep it consistent and also endeavour to make your morning routine something you can make into a solid habit that you won't give up.

6. **Take the power back from Social Media**

Note that I did not say: *'Delete your social media apps.'* Because there is plenty of merit in a digital detox, but you should delete every time-sucking apps that are of no value to you, social media can be very beneficial if properly put in used right in the right direction. Don't ever allow yourself to be taken over by the aimless scrolling on the phone and be left wondering where the last two hours went. Always endeavour to clean out your news feeds and leave only the ones that you find genuinely beneficial. Know that if it is not properly handled, the time it will take to do this will be more than earned back.

You should learn to re-examine your goals for success and therefore decide how you could utilize your social media to help further your goals of creating a successful habit.

7. **Make a Commitment to Achieve Every Single Day**

Make it a priority to have something done positively that will drive you towards achieving your goals. According to the Merriam Webster Dictionary, Commitment is an agreement or pledge to do something in the future. It also defines Commitment as a promise to be loyal to someone or something.

Decide to make a pledge today that you will have to do something everyday that will bring closer to exhibiting the habits of successful people and you will see yourself achieving it every single day.

8. **Take Control of Your Finances**

According to Wikipedia, Finance is a term for matters regarding the management, creation, and study of money and investments. It continues to state that specifically, it deals with the questions of how and why an individual, company or government acquires the money needed which is called capital in the company context and how they spend or invest that money.

Even though it may seem obvious, and you may think you are on top of your finances already, but we can all be guilty of bad spending from time to time. Even if you think it isn't compulsory, building a habit that is geared towards reviewing your monthly spending and deciding if there's a better way to distribute it for next month is an effective thing to do.

This is actually one of the easiest goals to reward yourself with. Because if you commit to saving a little extra money every month it can be used to give yourself a treat at the end of the year. Therefore, having a better grip on your own finances is a strong ability to have, and it's worth checking in regularly to make sure you are safe in the spending wagon.

9. **Surround yourself with Positive and Successful Individuals**

The quality of people that surrounds you will determine the quality of your results in life. If you show me the kind of friends you keep, I can also tell you the kind of outcomes you will produce. Because positive and successful people will bring out the positive and successful part of your life and negative people will bring out the negative side of you life. Every human being is just one person away from their goal, so if you must create the habit of success, you must surround yourself with successful people. If you have friends are people who have a tendency to draw back focus and distract you from your work, for example, you may ultimately need to make a choice between pursuing success and settling for your existing lifestyle. At this point I want to let you know that the idea of eliminating people from your life will make you feel uncomfortable, but ask yourself if your true friends would really risk your long-term happiness by actively trying to prevent you from achieving your goals.

10. **Maintain a Fit and Healthy Body**

Ignoring your health is a very big issue when it comes to creating a successful habit. One of the keys to building good habits is making your work to be sustainable. That's to say, you're not trying to do something big at once, but you're rather trying to form habits that can become part of your life permanently. One of such habits is taking proper care of your health. Like they it's always said, health is wealth. So the amount of health you enjoy will determine the amount of wealth you will also see.

Daily exercise should be part of your daily routine and visiting your medical professional for proper examination maybe monthly should also become part of your schedule as you plan the month. Make it a call of duty to take care of your health else your immune system will breakdown and that will lead to a very serious crisis that can eventually take your life. Whether it's walking, running, weight-lifting or swimming, endeavoring to inject a small level of exercise into your weekly routine will help you on the road to creating a successful habit.

11. **Be Prepared to Make Sacrifices**

According to the Merriam Webster Dictionary, Sacrifice is the act of giving up something that you want to keep especially in order to get or do something else or to help someone. It also continue to let us know that Sacrifice is to suffer loss of, give up, renounce, injure, or destroy especially for an ideal, belief, or end.

On your journey to creating habits that are going to be termed successful habits, you will be forced to make some sacrifices. One of such sacrifice is to devote to developing yourself on a continuous basis. Another is separate yourself from some people you feel are not helping you maintain your new habits and lastly, any activity that prevents you from doing your daily routine successfully should be avoided at all cause. As you are reading this timeless book now, I want you to always remember that there is a law called the law of sacrifice and it simply states that *"you cannot obtain something that you want without being willing to give something up in return."*, so you must therefore be prepared to also sacrifice a life of excess and material possessions in order to be successful in your career.

The proof of any new knowledge acquired, is in its application. And every proper application produces a well desired outcome. Having enumerated all these habits above, it is therefore subservient to know that having a short-coming in any of above mentioned habits, is a prove that you are heading to the domain of failure and a strict adherence to the above-mentioned is a road map to success. So it is therefore left for you to decide and choose which category you really want to belong, because it's only you that have the power to do that and no one else can do it for you.

# CHAPTER 8

## PERSONALITY TRAITS AND CHARACTERISTICS THAT GUARANTEES FAILURE OR SUCCESS

*"Personality is to a man what perfume is to a flower."*
**Paul P. Harris**

Having gotten a better understanding of what Failure and Success are earlier on in this timeless book, I will also want us to understand what Traits and Characteristics mean; so as to enable us grasp the full context of what we are talking about in this chapter of the book. It's a well-known fact of life that some people become successful and some people do not.

The question therefore is what makes one person to be able to achieve so much success when another person tries but experiences failure instead? Most times, the answer to this question can largely be found in the type of person that somebody really is, or more specifically, their own personality characteristics. This happens because the type of personality that you have has a massive influence over the direction your life goes in, because fundamentally, your personality dictates the type of thoughts you have which then determine the type of action you will take or will not take.

Breaking this down to the simplest level, it can be therefore, stated that your personality will either make it more likely for you to become a success, or less likely for you to becoming a success. Success is actually ahead of you, but you will only encounter it if you go down the right path. In this sense, success can therefore, be viewed as a by-product of your personality. It is also an end result of your most dominant thoughts and actions. So be careful what you think about or display therefore to people around you.

One of the biggest *"secret"* when it comes to what makes people successful, is that, their success came not from being more talented, smarter or luckier than the average person, but rather, it came because of the habits that they developed throughout the course of their life. The large majority of people in the universe for example, develop habits of failure as a direct result of their personality. Rather than working hard to achieve their own personal goals, they choose to do what is required to earn a living and survive, and then spend the rest of their time enjoying and entertaining themselves without any impact or value in mind.

The outcome of such lifestyle makes them to remain in more or less the same situation throughout their whole lives, this happens to them because, if you can't just do enough to get by, then be rest assured to fail because that's all you will ever do. Developing habits that leads to failure won't get you anywhere in life. Successful people on the other hand, take out their time to learn the personality or characteristics of success and failure, (which I recommend that you too should also learn), and they make sure that they spend the majority of their time and effort doing the things that will bring success into their life, rather than trying to engage the things which won't bring success to them.

Although the principle above may sounds simple, but it does require us having to make sacrifices, and at times, feeling lonely as we work hard to build up a successful future for ourselves. To achieve your goal of becoming successful in life, you must be willing to make the necessary sacrifice required to achieve it. But unfortunately, this is something that most people are unwilling to do or experience, which is why there are so many more unsuccessful people than there are successful people existing in the universe.

Now, what are the personality characteristics that we are talking about? Let's take a look at few of them now and find out:

1. **Being Lazy**

   According to Merriam Webster Dictionary, Lazy means to be disinclined to activity or exertion. It also means not energetic or vigorous.

If you are to be given a chance to make a choice today, on deciding the kind of life that you want to live, either by working hard all day or spending time having fun with friends and family? I think the answer should be very obvious! But been given a choice, most people would rather prefer to do something which is hard and necessary than just enjoying themselves with their friends and family. The reason for this is because; we should all learn and be driven by a desire to maximize our leisure time. This is an extremely important personality to recognize, because whenever you are given a choice, always learn to choose the easiest and quickest way to do that thing in order for you to maximize your leisure time.

A good example of how prevalent this tendency is can probably be found in our workplace. The large majority of our co-workers, for example, most likely can't wait to finish work, go home, have something to eat and then spend the rest of their day enjoying themselves in front of the TV or pressing their smartphones or computers. Actually, doing this things will not make you become successful, yet this is how most people spend the majority of their free time.

Every successful person on the other hand, has learnt to fight back against the natural urge to do what is fun and easy. They have also learnt that whilst having fun today may be enjoyable in the long run, it can result in them having less fun and enjoyment later on in their lives.

I want you to know that you may not always like what you have to do, but sometimes that's just the price you must have to pay for achieving your goals. The reason for this is because we are all lazy, and the vast majority of us like to stay that way because it's the easiest and most comfortable thing to do. No wonder why there seems to be so many more unsuccessful people than there are successful people in the universe. I want you to take note however, that being lazy isn't necessarily always a bad thing. But much of human progress, whether it's scientific or technological, has come as a result of a desire to get things done easier and quicker.

Let's take a look at the automobile for example; it was designed with the intention of getting people to where they wanted to go faster and without having to expend energy by walking. Today, much of modern-day society evolves as a result of the freedom that motor vehicles provided for us. Being lazy isn't always a bad thing per say, but much of human progress has come from finding more efficient ways to do things. So while being lazy can result in failure, it can also be a powerful motivation for success. Laziness in itself is not the problem, but the amount of laziness to be exhibited actually is!

*Action Step:* Always endeavor to learn how to overcome the urge to do what is fun, quick and easy all of the time. But choose instead, to do the things which are necessary, even if they are hard and will take a longer time to complete.

2. **Being Greedy**

According to the Merriam Webster Dictionary, Greedy means having or showing a selfish desire to have more of something (such as money or food). It also defined it as being very eager to have something.

One of the major causes of remaining unsuccessful is the desire to have more than you currently have. As a result of this you are never satisfied with what you have because you always wanting to have more. The greedy personality trait can quickly bring failure into your life, and this is one of the primary reasons why so many people are unable to save money and are always getting themselves into debt. I want you to also know that it is greed that now drives our consumerist society.

Just come to think of it. In the past, people used to be happy if they had something that worked and is helping them to do what they needed it to do. But today, however, functionality has become less of an issue, because now people are more concerned with the image of a particular product and how they think that others will view them for owning it than actually bringing products that will be solution to certain problems or challenges. This has eventually resulted in an endless variation of goods and brands that have been designed to target different consumer tastes and preferences. The here trouble is, that these tastes and preferences are always changing all the time, so if you must catch up with the trend then you must learn how to control this greedy characteristic, else you are going to spend a lot of money trying to satisfy your needs and that will certainly make you to remain in a state of being fruitless.

Many of our needs in life are fulfilled through material goods, but the satisfaction of these needs can therefore prove to be very expensive. So what then separates those who are successful from those who are not successful is not due to one being greedier than the other, but rather due to how greed is responded to by each parties. I have learnt a lot that unsuccessful people for example, tend to satisfy their needs immediately. In other words, if they see something they want they will try to get it as soon as possible, even if doing so has an undesirable consequence such as debt or making them spend beyond their budget. Successful people on the other hand, always respond to greed using a long-term time perspective. This means that they think about what they want, and then use the motivational energy that greed provides them with to work hard in order to get it achieved. Successful people use a well-defined vision of their future self to spur themselves forward through times of adversity. What I have also found out about successful people, is that the things which they have to wait for to get are often much more valuable and beneficial to their life than the things which they can get immediately.

Having this firsthand information, it then means that if you are always trying to satisfy your immediate needs, for example, watching TV instead of working, then in the long run, you probably aren't going to experience much success in life. So, I make bold to say that the most important point to remember here, is that greed in itself is not necessarily a bad thing, as the desire to have more is what makes society progress and get better as a whole. What determines whether greed is eventually beneficial or not, is what you do with it and when you do it.

***Action Step:*** Instead of trying to use greed for the satisfaction of your short-term needs, use the energy it gives you to help you work towards the attainment of the things that really matter and are important to you. Because these are the things that will eventually bring you success rather than failure.

3. **Being Ambitious**

According to the Merriam Webster Dictionary, Being Ambitious is having or controlled by ambition. It also defined it as having a desire to be successful, powerful, or famous.

Looking at it from the Collins Dictionary Online, Being Ambitious is having ambitions; eagerly desirous of achieving or obtaining success, power, wealth, a specific goal, etc.

Everything we do in the universe is motivated by a desire to enhance our quality of life. This can range from small short-term improvements, such as improving our mood of eating food, to larger long-term improvements, such as starting a small business and becoming financially independent. Even though we all are always trying to reach for something in life, there are some who choose rather to reach for more than others. Our desire to be Ambitious therefore is generally a good thing, as without being ambitious a person would never grow and advance in their life as they would always be doing the same things in the same place.

Unfortunately, however, most people in today's society are ambitious for the very wrong things. This is most times reflected by our focus on short-term improvements to one's life, we look at things that don't really matter in the long run. As a result of this, a larger majority of our society has been conditioned to expecting immediate results with the minimum amount of effort from their part. As you would have thought, this type of mentality is virtually guaranteed to bring failure into one's life. Successful people in other words tend to separate themselves from unsuccessful people by being ambitious for things in their long-term future, which as we have already mentioned, are also usually the things that will bring them the most benefit.

Real and genuine success comes from focusing on long-term goals, and then doing whatever it takes to complete them. So whereas an unsuccessful persons may concern themselves with who a particular celebrity is dating which has nothing to do with their success, successful people tend to focus their effort and energy on learning what they need to learn to help them achieve their goals at the right time.

***Action Steps:*** Decide today on the type of things that you are going to be ambitious about because they will largely determine the type of success that you will achieve in life, and the greater your ambitions are, the more of that success you are likely to achieve. Also endeavour to think about your main interests and ask yourself whether or not those things really matter in your life? Will they help you to achieve your goals and dreams? Or are they just leading you down a road towards long-term failure? Always be sure of what you doing at every given time.

4.  **Being Selfish**

According to Merriam Webster Dictionary, Being Selfish means to be concerned excessively or exclusively with oneself. It also defined it as seeking or concentrating on one's own advantage, pleasure, or well-being without regard for others.

In life, we all tend to act primarily from our own point of view. So the things we do therefore are done for the benefit of ourselves and not necessarily for other people. Most times even the act of charity is done with a selfish mindset. If you resolve to help someone, for example, it's usually because you feel some kind of passion for them. Once you have given help to them, it makes you feel better about yourself. This is why almost all the actions that we carry out in life are basically influenced by the feelings or emotions which we experienced and our desire to change them. Our actions are motivated by a effort to change our emotional state.

The implication of this is that due to our natural human tendency built to maintain a delightful state, or to move away from an unpleasurable state, this selfish desire can therefore cause a person to immediately want to change how they are feeling. This is done by doing something which is perceived as being more pleasurable than the existing action. People who fail in life tend to do so because they accept to give in to this desire immediately they encounter them, rather than doing the compulsory things first and then satisfying their desire later. For example, if a person doesn't feel like working and then go ahead to watch TV instead, that person is doing so because they know that it will bring them immediate gratification.

But I want you to know that a person who lives their life based solely by this principle is unlikely to ever get very far in life, because as you already know, most of the things that are worth doing require lots of time and effort on your behalf. So, in order to achieve worthwhile aims and objectives, you must be willing to put up with a certain amount of discomfort and also put other people in consideration before embarking on such actions or projects. It is from those discomforts that you will be motivated to work towards the attainment of something much greater and even brighter than you currently have. Sometimes you just have to experience a little pain to get that particular thing that you want out of life.

That is how successful people do their things. They are able to put aside their selfish desire and immediately change their emotional state by resisting meaningless activities and distractions. Always have this in mind and don't forget it in a hurry that *"the degree to which you are able to do this, will largely determine the success or failure that you will experience in your journey of life"*.

*Action Step:* Even though we are all driven by a desire to change our emotional state of mind. So if you don't feel like doing something, then that's usually a good indication that you should do it because doing so will bring the most benefit into your life and to the people around you. The more you can train yourself to do those things that were not willing to do, the more achievements you are likely to accomplish.

5. **Being Ignorant**

According to Wikipedia, the word Ignorant is an adjective that describes a person in the state of being unaware, or even cognitive dissonance and other cognitive relation, and can describe individuals who deliberately ignore or disregard important information or facts, or individuals who are unaware of important information or facts.

Looking at it from the Merriam Webster Dictionary, to be Ignorant means to be lacking in knowledge or information. It also described Ignorant as resulting from or showing lack of knowledge or intelligence.

Assuming that we are experts in something is what most times keep us perpetually in the state of failure. I want you to know that even Albert Einstein never knew everything about the subjects that he studied. The question now is, why do we often assume that we are experts on something? Because no matter how much time or amount you have spent to learn something, there is always more that you can still learn from that particular area or subject. So, in the true sense of life, we are all ignorant and carry out our actions based on our incomplete information. Our decision to recognize this characteristic can encourage us to become a lifelong learner, and thereby help us to avoid making the mistake of thinking that education stops once we finish our final exams at school.

Being a lifelong learner is very important in our today's society due to the fact that knowledge is constantly expanding at an ever-increasing pace. As a result, there is always more room for us to learn, and there is always more that we can do to try to improve our life and environment. There is always more that you can learn because nobody has the capacity to know it all.

It is only unsuccessful people that tend to stick with what they know. If they ever learn how to do something once, they will keep on doing it the same way for as long as possible until they are forced to make a change or quit that process. They are also very resistant to new information or instructions, because they feel that what they already know is just the only important thing and so there is no reason for spending their free time learning something extra. As a result this, they like to spend their free time watching TV, chatting on social media, reading celebrity magazines or playing games with their smartphones.

But what I want you to always remember that your decision to stop learning, does not make the world to stand still, that's for sure. Eventually, if you are not growing in your knowledge, talents and abilities, then know that your existing set of skills will also become obsolete. What then happens to obsolete people? They are always discarded and thrown to the side because they are no longer viewed as being useful or valuable enough to be worth keeping. So you need to constantly update your skills, so that one day you may not find yourself being thrown out into the dustbin.

If you ever contrast this type of character to the characteristics associated with successful people, you will find the complete opposite type of behavior. Because rather than thinking that they know everything, you will usually find out that highly successful people have a strong desire to learn every new information and to continually improve on their skills. As a result, you will always find them relentlessly reading or learning how to do something which they did not know or could not do earlier. Over time, it has been proven that such people are able to grow their knowledge, talents and abilities, and by doing so very well, they become more valuable to themselves and to other people around them.

*Action Step:* Just recognizing that what you know today will soon be outdated, positions you constantly to developing and improving yourself, because if you don't do that, you too will also become outdated.

6. **Having An Ego**

According to the Cambridge Dictionary, Ego is defined as your idea or opinion of yourself, especially your feeling of your own importance and ability. It also defined Ego as the idea or opinion that you have of yourself, especially the level of your ability and intelligence, and your importance as a person.

Ego has to do with our self-esteem. It determines how we feel about ourselves and what we think is possible or impossible for us to achieve. Low self-esteem which causes us to experience failure in our lives occurs as a result of a difference between our current self (i.e., the way we currently are) and our ideal self (i.e., the way we want to be). The wider this gap, the lower our self-esteem will be.

When dealing with failure, low self-esteem is something that's made worse by the society we live in, a society that constantly exposes us to wealthy and beautiful people in the media. When a person therefore compares themselves with such people, they seem to assume that there is a gap that exists between the celebrity and themselves. As a result, an average person looking at a celebrity can easily start to feel inadequate with who and what they are currently. People who exist with low self-esteem can become withdrawn due to feelings of inadequacy that were created by the media or the society at large.

Every person who operate with a low self-esteem is less likely to try anything new and challenging, this happens because they already have a believe system that tend to promote inadequacy and an expectation of failure. Low self-esteem individuals therefore prefer to stick with their familiar routines, and rarely get outside of their comfort zone. These kind of characteristics are obviously not going to make a person successful. In order to become successful, you must choose to work on raising your level of self-esteem by not allowing the media or any other factor in the society to make you feel inadequate with your current self. The easiest way this can be done, is to determine to work towards the achievement of your smart goals, because by doing so, you will automatically spend less time distracting yourself with what's on TV. You will begin to feel a lot better about your life if you spend most of your time doing things that add value to it instead of thing that don't add any value to your life.

In addition to that, you will also begin to find yourself becoming less interested with what's on TV, or what happening in the social media, as you will recognize these things as being of limited assistance or rather of no value in helping you to improve your life for the better.

*Action Step:* If you are currently suffering from low self-esteem, I want you to just recognize this fact and ask yourself this simple question

***'why I'm currently feeling this way'.*** Ask yourself again this questions, what is the reason for spending the majority of my time doing things that are wasting my life away? Or am I doing things that will help to bring success into my life? Answering those questions will programme you for a better and successful journey through life.

In conclusion of the above enumerated personality characteristics, I want you to know that the more worthwhile activities you do, the better you will feel about yourself and the better your life will turn out to be as a result of those activities.

**Some Traits Of Failure**

The truth of the matter is that not everyone is cut out for success, just like not everyone is cut out to become rich. I make bold to say this because no matter how you try to inspire or encourage some people to become successful, they will rather choose to remain in their current state of failure than decide to improve and become a better and valuable to their society. After several years of working with businesses, entrepreneurs, sales people and CEOs as a trainer and a coach, I have discovered that there are few traits that make people liable to to fail.

1. **Hate Being Told No:**

I'm yet to meet anyone that actually likes being told no, but if you tend to have a highly emotional response to being told NO and it sticks with you as part of your life, then success will be out of your reach. In fact, the universe will be unpleasant with you because you will be told *'NO'* by lots of people in many ways and many times. It is only the meaning that you place on the *'NO'* that will really determine how it will affect you. Your ability to learn how to turn a *'NO'* into *'YES'* will be critical to creating success.

2. **Unwilling To Ask For A Decision:**

I have come to realize that most people believe that once they can delegate things to others, it will help them in trying to avoid rejection and failure. They often try to hire others to handle this for them because they haven't developed the discipline of asking for a decision. But I want you to know that, being unwilling to ask for a decision from people, will always get you the leftovers and that is not good for a life that is determined to be successful.

3. **Believing Everything:**

If you are one of those that believe everything someone says to them is true, and that what people say is what they will do, your success is at risk. Because people will say many things to you that are almost meaningless; we are on a budget, we aren't buying, we are going to wait for the time being, I have to talk to my wife, and on and one. So, if you are not able to selectively listen, then it's possible you won't make it in your quest of becoming successful.

4. **Easily Sold On Another's Stories:**

   Don't be easily sold to believing other people's story. Because if you happen to be one of those personality types that is gullible and unable to maintain and communicate your conviction, then you are destined to fail. You will end up being stuck in some kind of reverse bounce back in the universe where in trying to convince another of your ideas and you end up buying their story instead.

5. **Unwilling To Reach Out Of Your Comfort Zone:**

   Being stuck to your comfort zone is a confirmed formula for remaining a failure. If you are therefore unwilling to reach out to people that are better connected than you, success will always be out of reach. Although, the people you know will be important, it is probably the people you have not yet connected with that can most likely help you out and help you to reach out of you to arrive at success. This will eventually require you to first, get out of your comfort zone and mix up with people you don't yet know.

6. **Believing Lowest Price Wins:**

> Believing that the lowest price is the reason people buy things, is perpetually keeping yourself in a state of suffering with cash flow and should please apply to become a clerk at either Shoprite or a waiter in a restaurant. 99.9% of all products on this planet can be replaced by cheaper alternatives. So, if a person wanted the lowest price, the best thing to do would be to not buy it at all. Always remember that price is actually a myth and not the reason people buy anything.

7. **Believing Persistence And Pressure Is A Bad Thing:**

> If you happened not to be one of those people that were in one way or the other convinced as a child by their parents, teachers, and environment that getting your way is a bad thing, then you should just throw away any success idea that you have. Because you need enough pressure to be able to stand in times of trial. A diamond is primarily only coal until the right amount of pressure is applied for the right amount of time. As a coach, I have also realized that people normally do not make decisions without someone insisting on it. Despising pressure or persistence will only take you forever to get your business working.

8. **Believing Selling Is A Negative Thing:**

The simple truth here is that, if you cannot sell then you cannot be successful. Because selling is your key to meeting and overcoming objections that will eventually come your way. So, your success therefore depends on this one ability probably more than any other single thing. I also want you to know that nothing happens without selling. If you think selling is wrong, unethical or something that someone else needs to do, then just be ready to be crushed, especially in this $21^{st}$ century economy. Every great success story that I have ever known or read about always had its core leadership path rooted to passionate and committed to selling.

9. **Believing The Economy Is The Problem:**

The economy is not really the problem but you are. Because the economy on its own is already problematic! Success is actually created over time, so during any run at success you will experience all types of economies. So, the person that makes the economy the variable for success will eventually become a victim to economic conditions at some point. Just have this in mind as we conclude this chapter that, successful people can create success in any economy and they also know how to use all types of economies to flourish in whatever they do to arrive at success.

Success as it is said earlier in this timeless book is not for everyone, but for those who are willing to do what it takes to get it. Most people just want it and are not willing to train and prepare for it. But if you are one of those people that think they are going to create success just because you have a good idea and are unwilling to train, invest and prepare for it, I can assure you that you will soon stumble. Everyone living in the universe has an idea but most people are not willing to develop their skills to the point that they can make that idea a reality! On my way to success I was plagued with a lot of competitive threats, industry changes, challenging economies and also find myself facing a lot of risk.

Let me sound this warning at this point in this timeless book, since the average worker reads less than one book a year and then wonders why they don't make it, you should not be one of those average workers. Strive to read at least a new book on your field of endeavour every month but if you can do more, read a new book every week. This will enhance and position you above existing as an average worker.

To ensure you become successful, always avoid the traits of failure and make it a dedicated commitment to learn everything you can about selling. Selling isn't a job, but a requirement for creating the success you want. Taking or engaging in sales trainings, sales motivation, daily sales meeting and the development of new sales skills will assist you in your journey of success more than anything else.

# CHAPTER 9

# REGRETS OF FAILURE OR SUCCESS

*"Never regret anything that has happened in your life,
Because it cannot be changed, undone or forgotten.
So take it as a lesson learned and move on with your life."*
**Joe O. Ikwebe**

According to Wikipedia, Regret is the emotion of wishing one had made a different decision in the past, because the consequences of the decision were unfavorable. According to it Regret is related to perceived opportunity.

Looking at it from the Merriam Webster Dictionary, Regret is sorrow aroused by circumstances beyond one's control or power to repair. It also defined Regret as to feel sad or sorry about (something that you did or did not do). It went ahead to explain that Regret is used formally and in writing to express sad feelings about something that is disappointing or unpleasant.

When it comes to choosing to attain success or failure, one of the vital things that we must consider before concluding this timeless book is Regrets. Regrets have made more people remain in failure than it has done to those that exist as success. You are going to be judged mainly by you level of maturity and ability to handle and absorb the amount of failures around you.

Becoming successful has a lot to do with your ability to overcome regrets in all its entirety. Failure is always surrounded with a lot of regrettable outcomes and thereby leaving you to remain in a state of thinking that someone or something was responsible for your failure whereas the true reality is that people only decide to regret the outcome of their past actions which most time establish them in a state of failure rather than that of success.

Regrets actually come in many forms either as failure or as a successful person. But the very first thing to do not to be held bond by the claws of regrets is to learn to overcome fear. Fear is the major causes of regret in the life of any person, business, family, organisation or career. Fear cripples the mind and makes it not to be able to take decisions that will lead to success thereby leaving you to regret your actions and outcomes later.

**Types of Regrets**

Having anchored some Business and Success Trainings and counseled a lot of start-up entrepreneurs, I have come to realize that there are two types of regrets generally. The first type of regret is ***Regret by Action*** and the second type is ***Regret by Inaction***.

## Regret by Action

Regret by Action happens as a result of decisions or choices that you made in the past. That is coming to a point where you begin to think that a certain decision or choice you made in the past brought or kept you in the situation that you are currently in. This form of regrets is what has made some people to remain at the state of failure and refusing to attempt something new that will eventually lead them to success. Regret by Action will make you to continually remember the wrong mistakes and steps you took in the time past that established you in failure. It has the capacity to deny you the access to new ideas and privileges that could project you to a successful endeavor.

One of the things this timeless book **"The Pride of Being A Failure"** was destined to create, is to provoke you to go back to those decisions, mistakes and actions you took in the past that has made you to think that success was not meant for you and redo all of them all over again and see if actually there was no success implanted in them for you to enjoy. Just take some time out of your tight schedules and revisit your past actions and mistakes that made you to fail and try redoing them again this time with a mindset that you are going to succeed and see if you will not actually succeed in that same thing.

What made you to fail all this time is not failure in its actual sense, but rather it is the fear of failure and the regrets that you think will occur from the decisions and actions that you are thinking to take. So, get up and try it one more time let's see what will be the outcome of it, because it could turn out to be the only thing you need to do to get to the top of that business, career, organisation or even ministry.

**Regret by Inaction**

Regret by Inaction happens as a result of not taking any actions or step. It is caused by a lack of decision. This is a state of regretting not doing anything at all in the past. I have realized that so many people who are thinking that they are failures today thinks that if they had taken some decisions or made some moves in the past, that things wouldn't have been as bad as it is now. But I want anyone reading this timeless book now that it is not too late to try as long as there is still breathe of life in you. The decisions and actions that you did not take or make before can still be made at this present time provided it is a good decision that will yield to success and not a fraudulent or illegal decision that will end you not just in prison but death.

When you think that things could have been different than it is now, if not for the actions that I refuse to take then the regret by inaction is at work and that has the capacity to keep you in a continuous state of not taking action or making any decision that will lead you to the path of success. So, if you want to overcome this type of regret, I want you to refuse to think of the actions you did not take and begin to think of the actions that you will take now that will actually lead you to the path of success.

Having taking some time to explain the types of regrets, I want to let you know that everyone regrets something and there's no shame in it. For me, one of the regrets that I always do is asking myself why this timeless book was not written earlier before now? I suppose to understand that the reason it was not written earlier is so that you who is reading this timeless book now will be ready and prepared to not just read it but decide to take action that will propel you to becoming and achieving success that will not just last with you but outlive you to other generations yet unborn.

Sometimes I take solace in the knowledge that everything I did, I just had to do it because it was geared towards bringing me to where I am right now. If I had taken another path different from what I'm doing right now, who knows where I'd be by now? Deep inside of me, I am a man overflowing with passion and desire and a need to love, be loved, help others, save the world, right wrongs, lead others toward great and wonderful things, and every day I think we can all lead satisfactory and even fulfilled lives this way. I want you to know that regrets actually are not living things but you are the one that is making them to look as if they are living things. Stop empowering them and they will automatically die out of your life.

# CONCLUSION

In conclusion of this timeless book ***"The Pride of Being a Failure"*** I want you to know that recovering from failure cannot be done with any form of perplexity or negligence. You must therefore be willing to Create or Develop a Massive Action Plan that will enable you to properly track your goals and visions. This will require you taking your goals serious and also endeavoring to lay out some definite action plans as to how you're going to achieve them. I you want to also learn and know what you will do in the face of failure next time when it rears its ugly head towards you.

Don't also forget this in a hurry that whenever we create or develop a massive action plan, it enables us to have a systematic way of achieving the goals that we set for ourselves. And once we come to the realization that those goals and visions won't be simple to achieve, we should then choose to approach things with a more durable way of achieving them so as to overcome any form of failure and this will lead us to a lifestyle that should enable us to attract success.

Always endeavour to set out a solid and massive action plan that will help you push past the stumbling blocks of life, and watch as you slowly but surely recover from any setbacks, upsets, or failure.

Failure will never be your portion again! No matter how far behind you are now, I see God bringing you to the front. Whatever you lay your hands to do henceforth will begin to speak for you. But don't forget that the only way to maintain the lifestyle of success is to acknowledge God as your source. As I mentioned earlier in this timeless book, God is the source of all wisdom. My prayer for you is for God to give you wisdom and the inspiration to excel and be successful so as to manifest the praises and awesomeness of God for men to see and acknowledge Him.

You are likely to be tempted to think that things are working because of your gift, talent or intelligence. Watch it! Never think that what you are doing now is moving forward because you are smart, otherwise, everything might crumble in no time. The higher you go, the more you need to humble yourself. Build around yourself some personal principles that will help you to remain cool and focused to God.

You must do everything to keep away from pride. Because it corrupts mentality, it turns your mind backwards and you end up in foolishness rather than wisdom. What makes you successful is not your effort, it is God. So do everything to keep Him on your side.

Avoid regrets of any form because it will rather draw you backward instead of pushing you forward. I want you to also know that what made you to fail all this time is not failure in its actual sense, but rather it is the fear of failure and the regrets that you think will occur from the decisions and actions that you are thinking to take. So, get up and try it one more time let's see what will be the outcome of it, because it is very possible that it could turn out to be the only thing you need to do to get to the top of that business, career, organisation or even ministry.

Also remember that as a Coach, my duty here in this timeless book *"The Pride of Being A Failure"* is to provoke you to go back to those decisions, mistakes and actions you took in the past that made you to think that success was not meant for you and redo all of them again and see if actually there was no success embedded in them for you to enjoy. Please endeavor to take some time out of your tight schedules and revisit your past actions and mistakes that made you to fail and try redoing them again this time with a mindset that you are going to succeed and see if you will not actually succeed in that same thing.

Always endeavour to be the original person God intended you to be. Don't settle for anything less. Don't look back, look forward and decide today to take steps toward His plan for your life. And remember that it's a thing of pride to have the privilege of being a failure before becoming successful because that actually what is going to guide you throughout you journey of success.

# EPILOGUE

Having gone through this timeless book, you must have realized the great price involved, in the quest of becoming a Success and also the danger of ending as a Failure. Nothing of value is free. If therefore, success is all about service, then it must carry a definite cost.

My attempt in this book has been, to unfold the diverse cost involved in becoming a Failure or a Success. Value is essentially a function of cost. It is time to stand up to the challenge and give the success in you a chance of expression.

The top is very open and free, but everyone has to make his way there. It is time to sit up, so you can stand out in you successful and impactful lifestyle. It is time to fasten your seat belt, so you can go fast and far. It is time to brace up, so you can fly high.

This timeless book is about helping you to accept full responsibility, for the success dreams of a genuine and great service provider that you have. It was Martin Luther King Jnr. that said, *"Whatever affects one directly, affects all indirectly. I can never be what I ought to be until you are what you ought to be. This is the interrelated structure of reality."* So, if this book succeeds in putting you on the right cause of your destiny, then my purpose for writing it would have been fulfilled.

I have realized that one of life's beautiful truths is that you can accomplish anything you have ever dreamed of accomplishing within a given time frame. All you need to accomplish any task, is the bridge that will connect where you are currently and where you want to be in the future.

So if you have read anything in this timeless book that you want a better understanding, then I would like to talk to you. Call today for your full information on booking **Joseph O. Ikwebe** for your corporate seminars, conferences, meetings, coaching and consulting @ **+2347037774042, +2348124472230** or email: joeoikwebe@gmail.com, Twitter@joeikwebe

You can also send me mail on how this book affected your life and other suggestions if you have any. Thank you for spending your precious time reading this book. I wish you tremendous success and true happiness, and I look forward to meeting you in person.

**Joseph O. Ikwebe.**
*Social Entrepreneur & Life Coach*

www.ingramcontent.com/pod-product-compliance
Lightning Source LLC
Chambersburg PA
CBHW060849220526
45466CB00003B/1304